Search Engine Optimization All-in-One SEO For Dummies

A Complete book with Steps to Search Engine Optimization Success on Google

Hemanta Saikia

Green Booker Publishing

Copyright © 2016 Green Booker Publishing

All rights reserved.

ISBN-13:978-1540628428

ISBN-10:1540628426

DEDICATION

To my Parents, wife Emi Kalita and other family members.

CONTENTS

Chapter:1	SEARCH ENGINE OPTIMIZATION (SEO)	3
Chapter:2	KEY WORDS RESEARCH	11
Chapter:3	CONTENT OPTIMIZATION	25
Chapter:4	TECHNICAL SEO	39
Chapter:5	LONG TERM PLANNING	52
Chapter:6	LINK-BUILDING STRATEGIES	70
Chapter:7	EFFICIENCY OF SEO	81
Chapter:8	ECOMMERCE	90
Chapter:9	LOCAL SEARCH	101
Chapter:10	INTERNATIONAL SEO	115

ACKNOWLEDGMENTS

I would also like to give my special thanks to my family whose patient love enabled me to complete this work. I extend due respect and gratitude to all those who helps and co-operations will be valuable and precious for all time to come before me.

CHAPTER:1
SEARCH ENGINE OPTIMIZATION (SEO)

The web has basically changed the way we live and the first page popped up on the World Wide Web first page become a dream for everyone. Next to email, we do most within internet is the search; because search is really the doorway to everything else we do online. As a business, it's no longer good enough to just be online these days you have to be found. While SEO can become very technical and complicated; in this book we will focus on the fundamentals of SEO. We will talk about how to find them, research the keywords that you want your pages to rank for, how to come up with an optimized content for that keywords, and the importance of links from other websites and social exposure. We will discuss the concepts and will dive into some code and along the way will touch on e-commerce, local and even international considerations. Lastly, we will focus on measurement strategies that can help you understand just what you're doing back from your investment in search engine optimization. The Internet is now simply a part of her everyday lives as consumers we rely on search engines to show us what were looking for.

WHAT IS SEARCH ENGINE OPTIMIZATION (SEO):

Search engine optimization is the process of making improvements on and off your website in order to gain more exposure in search engine results. In more exposure in search engine results will ultimately lead to more visitors finding for the right reasons and going to your website. In order to understand what improvements will affect search engine results let us take a step back and understand the goal of the search engines themselves. At the heart of it search engines are just annoying to locate and recognize all the content out there on the web & then rapidly deliver relevant and authoritative results based on every phrase of user might be searching for. First let's talk about relevance, when a user searches for something like Delhi hotels, search engines want to show list of results that are relevant to the topic of Delhi hotels. Search engines analyze all the web pages they ever visited and pick up the pages of the believer the most relevant to Delhi hotels. They determine this by evaluating lots of different factors as well as how your substance is written & put into practice in code in addition to how other websites around the Internet or linking to you and all of these is stuffed into a very good very complex and very proprietary algorithm. At the end, a search engine is then able to rank and displayed all of those web pages in order of relevance to that phase the user just type to Delhi hotels. This is very significant to appreciate since search engines create a very obvious difference amid continents about Delhi hotels versus Continental relevant for other phrases like Delhi resorts or phase like travel getaway. Search engines were able to understand about semantic and thematic connections between words and concepts. Take another example dog crates; search engine knows the pages selling dog-cats are extremely relevant to that search query but also knows that websites about pet carriers are also very relevant. It also knows that a website promoting things like pet food and dog toys might also be relevant to the search word; perhaps less so. The other factor that influences search engine exposure is authority. In other words out there in the large wolves World Wide Web where anyone can post anything is your website or trusted place on the Internet that the search engines would want to show to their users. One very common way that search engines determine the authority of a webpage or domain is by evaluating what other websites think of you and this can be measured through the links out there, reporting to your website. A link is a vote on the Internet. A webpage linking to your website is almost like saying as "hey we trust your content enough that I'm willing to reference your page" and possibly even sent traffic to your site. It's a vote of trust. Search engines pick up on this as they clean the web reading, evaluating and storing all data they find on all the pages on internet. But it is important to know that this is not just a popularity contest were you trying to accumulate the most votes on the Internet. Search engines have safeguards in place to prevent this kind of mistreatment & in its place an stress on the excellence of the link; for example a search engine is more likely to trust a link if it comes from a well respected or industry related site like an industry-leading blog or a nonprofit or government agencies that's involved in your field of work. A link coming from a one-month-old site that has nothing to do with you or your industry and not going to be valued nearly as much. From the search engine's perspective, some links are more effective than others in casting their vote to your website and determine your sites authority. So you might think of this whole system is weighted democracy where some votes are worth more than others. Both relevance and authority is important to a search engine which help us to both understand and improve these factors and will ultimately lead to better search engine exposure and more visitors to the pages of our websites.

SEARCH ENGINE RESULTS:

Before discussing your website to show up in the search results, it's important to understand what those search results actually look like. Although there are many search engines around the world & they all have some separate dissimilarity. There are some common characteristics of the search engine results pages or search may have. One thing that we are probably going to find some paid listings. Paid listings are very different than the traditional organic or natural listings that will be focusing on for SEO efforts. These paid listings are actually advertisements and programs like Google's Adwords are Microsoft Ad Center allow advertisers to bid on and place these Ads in the search results page.

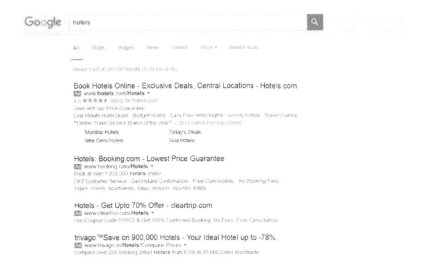

A typical search engine results page will have ten organic results that link out to different web pages. Each result might look a little different but though all have at least the headline the description and a visible URL. It's important to know what these components look like. The Internet has changed a lot since search engines first appeared. There is a lot of content on the web beyond just text in web pages. Search engines have done a good job of keeping images and well we still view webpage results they've also

Search Engine Optimization

begun returning things like video, images, products and maps on a search engine results. An ordinary way of telling this would be that we have merged search results that include all kinds of different content.

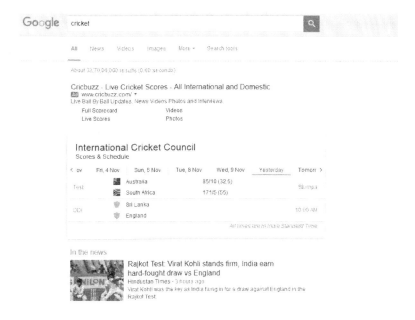

Sometimes the blended results will have a group of video clips that match a user search query or it might show a list of local businesses accompanied by a map. It could be a group of images and prices for a particular product that you can purchase. Social signals permit search engines to revisit more modified consequences like news, articles that your friends of shared. These results can show up in a variety of diverse ways based on what the search engines believe is applicable and suitable to the user searching query. The important thing to remember is that you have a lot of opportunities to have your contented show up in the search engine and the more you appreciate how search engines decide to show results to users, the more you understand how to get the search engines to show your content above the rest.

SEO FOR BUSINESS STANDARD

If you are in business, there are some very real and very specific benefits to having a consistent ongoing search engine optimization strategy. For the first time, users are offering up the actual intent through the wisely type of the search engines and more than ever before you can measure the efforts as a marketing channel. While search engines don't charge for listing your web pages; planning and implementing SEO in your organization is certainly not free. You'll need to spend the time, money and the resources to do this the right way. The good news is that this can help you obtain a tremendous marketing reach, attract more targeted visitors and measure the impact of your efforts in terms of return on your investment. More and more content appears on the web every second of every day and your customers needs search engines to help make sense of it. In fact the bigger the web gets, more search engine usage keeps growing year after year. People search to find answers to your questions to buy products to find a place to travel to get news just about everything we do online, starts with search and is not just in family PCs anymore. The explosion of connected mobile and tablet devices means that we are access to search, just about anywhere in the world. What people search for is a lot about their intentions or what actions they intend to take a specific moment in time and this is traditionally been the holy ground of market research. If somebody searches for mobile deals in India where the buyer digital camera, it's very easy is as a marketer to understand and react to what they're looking for. The role of search engines is to match those users search quarries to pages that match the topic and if you sell cameras that means to you create relevant content that meets the needs of researcher at exactly the right moment. Good SEO to essentially provide you a stream of some of the most targeted intentional traffic you could possibly ask for. More than about one of the biggest benefits of search engine optimization is the ability to actually measure your results. You can use your website analytics data to find out exactly how successful you are in acquiring search engine users and you can see if those users' actions were in line with your business goals. You can evaluate the effectiveness of your content and attracting in advancing the users through your sales funnel and you can measure what to do and what they don't too on your website. By attaching real money and sense to those actions that began with a simple search, you will be able to truly measure the return on investment.

SEO OUTLOOK:

Search engine optimization is a process and requires a lot of work, a lot of time and a lot of patience. It's important to set some expectations. SEO is a bit different than most other marketing strategies and understanding these differences will help us to guide encores for running a measuring successful SEO campaign. Patience is a virtue and that could not be truer than with SEO. An approach is a long-term process of building long-term value. There is a reason that all in rank number one in Google tomorrow scams are called scams. It takes time to develop and execute on your strategy to researcher keywords to create new sole content to construct additional links and more power and to decide any technical issues with site and is a never ending process. SEO is not a one-time project; it's a process you continue doing for the lawful. You also want to keep in mind that search engines don't necessarily interact with your website immediately. They take some time to discover changes your content, new links to your pages, overall structure of your website and will take more time to put all those factors in their algorithms to re-assess your relevancy and authority for those changes are reflected in the search results. Being patient and true to your strategies will help you stay focused on SEO process that was laid out. Another important thing with

SEO is to show change within the search engines and it is important to realize and accept that; we have no control over this. Search engines are always trying to improve their product to help deliver results that people want and they always trying new things. Sometimes changes are algorithmic; other changes are more about futures i.e. different ways of presenting different kinds of content to users. Search engines will keep making changes to enhance the experience for their users; so it's in our best interest to work with the changes is best we can do. One of the biggest expectations for successful SEO campaign is to realize that you really optimizing for two audiences: search engine and real human beings. It's really easy to focus on what with the search engines will akin to site. But the genuine interview that makes business on your website is people. What we may never find us if we don't show up on the search engine results page, its people who drive the bottom line and the fortunate thing is the search engines know that. Search engines have the ultimate goal to generate search results that people find useful and helpful. If you build your authority, create content that is interesting to people and if you do it in a way that's friendly to the computerized audiences well the long-term and consistent goal of the search engines is to reward that.

****

CHAPTER: 2
KEY WORDS RESEARCH

Before you can optimize your website you need to know what you are optimizing for. Finding the right keywords to focus your SEO efforts on can be challenging; fortunately is a lot of data out there in a structured approach that we can use for our keyword research. Keywords are what searchers type into a search engine; search engines like Google and Bing will go out and fetch the most relevant results for your search quarry based on everything they know about you and all the content on the entire Internet. But, it's important to remember that search engines have a hard time understanding what users really after and spelled-out. This is why you probably followed up one search with another more descriptive search more than a few times in her life. You try one keyword but it doesn't give you just were looking for. So, you get more specific or you tried another way. The bottom line is that people all over the world are typing in all kinds of keywords every second of every hour of every day and it's important for us to understand what to type in; so that we can optimize your pages to be search results. Keyword research is the opening part in SEO that will help you understand what people are typing into search engines? How frequently they do it? All relevant those terms are to your business objectives and how competitive those terms will be to try to rank for; for example say, you sold cars, you might think of the keyword car is something that you are right forth, but after you do a little keyword research you probably find of the way you make your list; why? Even though that were just typed in the search engines with a very high frequency, think about its relevance. How many reasons could someone type the word car in search engines and they might be looking for a toy cars or repair cars or rental cars. Hundreds of things are there that have nothing to rank for the word car in the search engine. This is an extremely competitive term or phrase like buy, used Toyota Car might not get as much but it's extremely relevant and probably not the competitive. Keywords like this will very likely end up on your list of keywords to optimize for. Now we understand a bit more about keywords & keyword investigate, it's occasion to speak about planning. An effectual keyword research plans alternative sound instructional approach that will lead to the discovery of keywords that you can use them at content of your website. Ultimately a keyword research plan will give you the data you need to make decisions about which keywords will give you the biggest bang for your buck and have the highest likelihood of being both relevant and profitable for your business. With billions of words searched each month, it's important that we understand the goals of the keyword research process what were looking for and how we collect and analyze the data to make decisions on our website.

Search Engine Optimization

RESEARCH KEYWORDS:

Everyone will eventually develop their own approaches and process to drink keyword research and you ultimately need to find something that works for you. But the most important part of keyword research is to forget about your business and put yourself in the shoes of your potential customers. The process typically begins with brainstorming and answering some key questions. It is important from an managerial viewpoint as it will force you to look at diverse areas of your business start with answering what services do you offer? Be as comprehensive as possible and list out as many keywords and phrases you can but make sure that you do it from a customer's perspective. As people who worked in organizations that are you in and day out we might have a very different way of explaining our products and services; take for example the discount travel website; you might be tempted to write down keywords like high-value or transport, discount ticket but at the end of the day no one in the world is type embedded with search engine. While those things make sense to you; your customers are just looking for things like cheap flights. Brainstorming can get you started. We look at some tools that are confined and suggest similar keywords and expand your list of possibilities considerably. Once you got the list of potential keywords the next thing is to do was take a look at the search volume metrics to see what kind of demand for those phrases. As you do this you'll notice that a handful of keywords typed in thousands and thousands of times a day but there are a whole lot more they are targeting nearly as often. These might be more descriptive keywords with less common variations but the important thing to note is that these are known as long tail keywords. Long tail keywords and SEO are incredibly useful and let us go about much larger amount of less competitive keywords that attend to be extremely relevant to our business objectives and will individually there is not a lot of search volume of each term the each to have some search volume. For example if I were showing iPhone cases I may start looking into the keyword iPhone cases. It's extremely competitive and it's probably going to be very difficult to rank for but I might also take a look at a more long tail keyword like blue iPhone cases. It's going to be extremely relevant less competitive end-user to run for at the expense of raw search volume. But here's the important part of you will find hundreds or thousands of these long tail keywords that together have the potential to get you more traffic than writing for iPhone cases would have from start. Finally you want to add some meaning an organization around the keywords you have collected. You may do this by recognizing themes or subject to cluster your keywords about; a procedure known as keyword categorization. Back to the example with the blue iPhone case, we may want to create a group it will be just about blue iPhone cases that includes all the different models of the iPhone. Alternatively we could categorize these by full model; but instead by colour: there is no right or wrong way to do this; only works for you and allows you to manage these groups of keywords as you optimize for them. But this is an exploratory and discovery exercise and everyone searches differently and you will find lots and lots of data as you dig deeper and deeper; be open-minded which results in the mindset of your potential customers and make sure to consider all of your options as your evaluator keyword performance over time.

TOOLS TO ANALYZE KEYWORDS

Now that we understand the basics around how we conduct keyword research. Let's dive into the tools that will help us find more keywords and collect all the data will need while there are quite a few tools out there perhaps the one that gets the most use is the Google keyword tool. Not only this tool provide a good measure on search volume but improvements on keyword suggestion has made it a more favorable keyword research tool in the SEO community and the best part about it is that it's free. While you don't need to be an Adwards advertiser to use this tool; if you do have an ad words account to get access, you might consider signing up for a free account. From Adwords you can access this tool from the tools and keywords planners. There are three keywords search types:

► Search for new keywords using a phrase, website or category
► Get search volume data and trends
► Multiply keyword lists to get new keywords

Before we do research let's take a look at some of the options that we can use by opening the 'Search for new keywords using a phrase, website or category' options and filters area you can choose to see data for the entire world or just the countries you select and you can also choose the language of your keyword results. Here we have chosen the United Kingdom. Another important selection is the devices that people are searching on. The kinds of key words people type into their mobile phones are often a lot different than the ones at the type into desktops or laptops and you can see the differences by using the selection as you do your research. Last you can choose to filter your results for things like certain levels of competition or search volumes. Over on the left you want to select a preferred match type. Ad words advertisers are familiar with these types; but for our purposes will make sure that there's a check and only the exact matchbox, which will ensure that were getting data for only the keywords were looking at exactly as they appear. Now ready to get started and there are a few ways we can do it first, we can type one or more keywords into the word or phrase box by entering them one per line you can also choose to enter a website URL and the tool will go crawl the page to try and find relevant keywords. For now will keep things simple and just type in iPhone cases and click get ideas.

[Screenshot of Google Keyword Planner showing keyword suggestions for iphone cases, including iphone 5s cases, iphone 4 cases, iphone 4s cases, iphone covers, waterproof iphone case, iphone 4 cover, iphone 4s covers, and best iphone cases with their average monthly searches, competition levels, and suggested bids.]

As you can see the Google keyword tool is a great suggestion tool from his one term we start to discover that people are also searching for things like best iphone 5s cases, iphone 4 cases and waterproof iphone case. Over on the right you can choose which columns of data you want to see. Global monthly searches includes the entire world if you specified a country in your settings the local monthly searches will only show data for the countries your selected. You'll also want to make sure the competition is checked in the local search trends column can give you some interesting insights into seasonality. Right from this tool you can select the keywords that you want to potentially including your keyword list and you can download a list of the raw data in CSV format where you can work with the data off-line and tool like Excel. Remember that this tool was developed for Adwords advertisers and as such there are more options that we haven't talked about that have to do with Adwords and not necessarily SEO. Spend some time with this tool and dig around for lots and lots of keyword ideas and data. Another great tool to get even more information about a keyword is Google trends for search which can be found https://www.google.com/trends/. This lets you type in different keywords and see all kinds of information about how that keyword is being typed into Google searches overtime. Over on the right you can filter this data by type of search geography time period and even category. Let's stick iPhone cases in here and see what we can learn. Here we see a graph of how this term is good search for over the years, along with key pieces of news that can help us figure out what might have caused certain spikes or troughs.

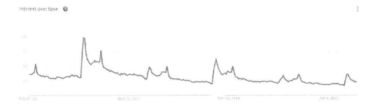

while there's been a pretty good upward trend over the years across the world. Let's get a little more specific and select just the United Kingdom for the last 12 months and let's compare it to the singular version of this keyword iPhone case.

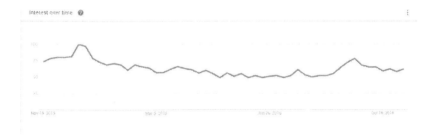

Here we can see exactly what our demand picked up and we can see that more people are typing in the singular version than the plural. Scrolling down we can see state-by-state interest to the heat map and below that we can get even more keyword ideas in the top and rising searches section. Putting some of these back into the keyword tool can start a whole new iteration of research. Using tools like the Google keyword tool, Google trends for search allows us to discover new keywords and understand just what people are typing into search engines. This exploration and data collection is the backbone of our keyword research process and can provide us with wonderful insights and ideas around which keywords will focus on as part of our SEO strategy.

KEYWORD ATTRIBUTES

There's an enormous amount of data available to us about the keywords people are typing into search engines and it's important to be able to evaluate the different attributes of the keyword before we decide whether or not to target one whether SEO strategy. There are three things you need to think when deciding your keywords: relevance, search volume & competition.

Relevance the first thing you need to do when you're deciding whether keywords relevant to your business are to ask yourself one simple question. Does the keyword you found accurately reflect the nature of the products and services that you offer? If so you've nailed it. One task of a search engine is to find the most applicable content to its users for a given search term. The best way to understand your customers search behavior is to put yourself in their shoes. If you were in the market to buy a car how would you use a search engine? You probably wouldn't type the word car in and click search. Instead you do something very specific to what you're looking for like: used Toyota. Now if you're selling used Toyota and you have a page on your website dedicated to them than that is a relevant keyword and the best part about relevant keywords isn't they much more likely to drive conversion actions on your website then the more generic once. The second item to look at is the search volume. While used Toyota might be extremely relevant to your business and likely to lead to a sale. It's also not typed into a search engine all and often search volume is the number of searches per month for a particular keyword and if you use a tool like the Google keyword tool, it is represented as the average number of searches for the last 12 months. Because this number is a rolling average seasonality and other trend patterns are not accounted for. If your business is seasonal you'll want to take a look at the local trends, column in the keyword tool or even Google trends for search when analyzing your keywords. Now let's have a look at the competition and what we mean by this is essentially? just how difficult it's going to be for us to rank in front of our competition on a search engine results page? unless you're introducing a new product or technology to the market, you're probably going to find continent similar to yours already on the web and we can look at things like the number of pages about a given topic authority and trust of the websites competing with you back links to their websites and more. One way to look at this is by evaluating the keyword in the paid search or cost per click markets. The number of search advertisers actively bidding on a keyword can be a good proxy for just how difficult the keywords going to be on the organic side and the Google keyword tool has a competition column that shows you this. The SEOmaze keyword difficulty tool can be another good source of keyword competition data. This tool will analyze keywords and figure out how difficult it would be to rank well in search engine results based on the strength of pages and websites listed in the search results. Let's tie altogether by going back to our car example when we say car versus used Toyota. We might find that there are lots and lots of the specific types of keywords that don't get a lot of volume but are very relevant to our used car dealership and not very competitive. Keywords like used Toyota or used blue 2010 Toyota or use Honda Accord might not give us a lot of volume; together we could be drawing lots and lots of relevant likely to convert visitors to our website.

KEYWORD DISTRIBUTION

Keyword distribution is the procedure of transmission keywords to precise pages on your website. This is an important step in the content creation process and results in the content on a page being aligned & applicable. Once you have recognized all your target keywords through the keyword research process, we found that working in Microsoft Excel or another spreadsheet allows you to create your site structure in an organized way and it has the added benefit of keeping a record of which pages are targeting which keywords to refer back to in the future.

Search Engine Optimization

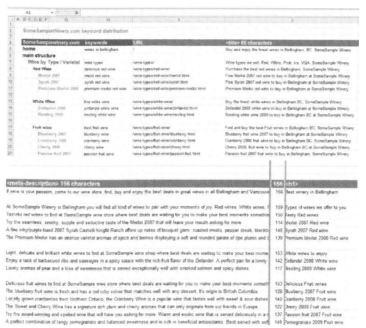

Keep in mind that for many of your target keywords you won't get have a page and you'll need to create one by using a spreadsheet, you can easily see where in your site's architecture you want to put it and define some key pieces of information about it before you even start writing. Here is an example of a spreadsheet we created for a fictitious sample winery. You can format your spreadsheet anyway you like, but there are some common fields that you should include; down the left-hand side we like to use cells or tabbing to show pages of our site. As you can see for each page, we have a column for the keyword will be targeting on this page, the URL of the page, the title tag the meta-description, and the H1 header. We even used excels link function to count our characters so that we can see how close we are to or general targets. Again our title of 65 characters for a title and 156 characters for description are not hard limits by any means. It will avoid search engines truncating this information on the search engine. The first step is to inhabit the spreadsheet with your accessible web pages. Be sure to include every page of your site including your home page, about page, location page, contact page another general kinds of content pages. Remember search engines want to see unique information for each and every page. In listing them all out here is a good way to quickly spot any duplication. The second step is to take a look at the keywords from your keyword list and find the most appropriate pages of your site for each of the keywords. You should make sure to distribute one keyword per page and try not to force anything. Remember search engines prefer unique and relevant content. So, if you have a keyword that doesn't match any page of your site you want to create a new page. When you add a new page to your spreadsheet the good news is that you've got a blank canvas. You can define the SEO friendly URL, title, description and header right here in the spreadsheet. Writing content when you know the keyword you're optimizing it for upfront allows you to really dial in on all the best practices of content writing for keywords that will be covering. Remember the meat of each page is the body copy and you'll probably need to go back through your existing pages to make sure that there really optimized for the keyword you defined as a target. Now, that you got your target keywords in mind; now is a pretty good time to head over to one of the on page analysis tools. It will talk about a little later in this book. The suggestions from these tools can really help guiding the changes, you'll be making to your pages. Using a keyword distribution spreadsheet will help you in a number of diverse ways. First it provides you one place to systematize & document the content of your site that will support the keywords that you're targeting. Second, it serves as an excellent resource for your copywriters & will help rationalize workflows across all the different members of your website production team.

Search Engine Optimization

Ongoing keyword evaluation:

Ongoing keyword evaluation is critical to the long-term success of your SEO efforts and it's really the last step of the keyword research cycle. With all the great keyword data that we can look at, the one data point that we can find out about those keywords is how they actually perform for us. Once we start ranking for the keywords we targeted and we start to get traffic coming to our pages as a result of those search engine rankings, we will need to see if those keywords are actually driving conversion actions in business objectives. Remember that used Toyota keyword that we thought would be so perfect for us. While it might turn out that everyone typing that keyword and was search engine is looking for a place to take the car to get fixed for free as a result of some product recall. All of our research told us that this would be a good keyword but it might turn out that it's not driving in car sales.

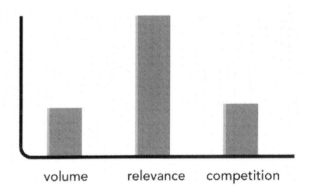

The point is will need to be able to adapt. you'll find that some keywords to start producing results for you and don't be afraid to swap in new keywords in place of those that are working and you only notice once you've already got traffic coming to your site from those keywords. A quick way to do some testing is through paid search. Using Google ad words or Microsoft ad Center you can buy the keywords that you want to evaluate for a short period of time and collect the data that will help you understand whether or not these keywords are going to provide business value for you. While paid search clicks do tend to behave a little differently than clicks on organic search results. This can be good proxies and potentially save you months of work and lost opportunity and don't forget that SEO isn't just a onetime set it and forget it project it's a continuous process and has to be maintained over the long term. This industry is constantly changing and the way people use search engines is evolving too. The keyword research that you did a year ago might not be valid anymore. So make sure that you're revisiting this exploration a few times a year to find new opportunities. By staying abreast of changes with fresh research and focusing on how your target keywords contribute to your website organic traffic and business objectives. You'll be developing a better understanding of your visitors, their search patterns and how you can serve them better with the pages of your site month after month and year after year.

****

CHAPTER: 3
CONTENT OPTIMIZATION

Content optimization is the process of improving the quality and relevancy of your sites content. We will discuss a number of things about how both users and search engines interpret what makes good content. But first let's go through a few examples of how human beings might read a piece of content and figure out what it's all about. Let's take a look at the example of backpacking in Thailand. Let's pretend that someone gave us a one page document and they told us of the document was about backpacking in Thailand. We read some text describing some landmarks along the Coast of the Thailand. We see some pictures of oceans & beaches and parking policy along the sides.

Now this might be about backpacking in Thailand but reading the document, it's not very clear. You put the page down and you're probably disappointed. Even if the exact phrase backpacking in Thailand was used in the text here, it was all over the place and there's really no central theme to focus on. Both people and search engines expect clarity and quality from your web pages. They want to know without any hesitation what your content is all about and even more importantly they want content they can trust. if I ask you to find me a resource on backpacking in Thailand and you come back with a piece of paper with a few mentions of the term in some text it's loosely related to landmark some things about the state of Thailand are not can I ask you next time or if I do, not to trust you as much. On the other hand, if you give me content it's truly remarkable discussing how to backpack the role those Thailand landmarks with maps and hiking guides descriptions of Thailand flora and fauna that you might see while backpacking and reviews of Thailand backpacking trips from other hikers. I come back to you with more questions in the future and greater trust your answers. In the online world, when people find content they like they share it. Search engines can see a lot of the sharing and they view it as a sign of trust and will reward you with more search engine visibility. We think about content optimization

Search Engine Optimization

keep in mind that were optimizing your content, so that it benefits both users and search engines and were focusing on both theme and building trust.

OPTIMIZING SITE STRUCTURE

As you focus on more and more key words and themes, you'll be developing more content on your website and you'll start out a lot of pages to hold this content. It's going to be important to structure all these pages in a meaningful way because in order for search engines to return your pages to searchers in response to relevant search queries, they need to understand how your pages relate to one another. let's imagine you are visiting a bookstore for the first time, you're looking for a fiction book written by an author whose name starts with the letter J. since this is the first visit you don't know where anything else and you have to learn the layout of this new bookstore. Fortunately, the bookstore has some really good navigation to help you out. You look at the store directory to find where the fiction section is located. Once you reach the fiction section, you identify the specific that has fiction books written by authors whose names start with a J. You then look at that section and you find a specific book you are looking for. Now imagine you keep going through this procedure to study the whole layout of the bookstore. You may form out all the diverse sections, categories and authors and eventually you'll end up knowing about all the individual books. This is exactly what a search engine does. It crawls the entire website to learn what's there, how it's organized, where exactly all the content can be found and what it's all about. Now imagine that instead of simply visiting a bookstore, you know work at the bookstore, you've learned everything about how the story is laid out and where specific books are. If a customer walks in the door and says, I am looking for a fiction book written by an author whose name I can't remember but I know it starts with the letter J, you'll be able to immediately guide them to the book you're looking for. Now you or the search engine people come to you looking for information and you point the way to it and you can do this quickly and efficiently because you have unspoken the contented and how it's prearranged. A search engine will discover your homepage and start another do through your website through your links. The way you like to pages within your own site, it is important and it's known as internal linking. If you're an online store for example, you might have a system of product categories that went to subcategories that grasp links to personnel products. If you have an informational site, you may be prearranged by topics, dates of publication. Whatever structure and strategy you choose a clean site structure will really help search engines appreciate your whole website, discover content and assist searchers find what they're looking for. On the other hand, a bad site structure can be detrimental to research engine understanding your site. You might find websites that have no navigation at all or force you to scroll for hours for a single page, single tier site map to find what you are gazing. You might watch links that obtain users down. We might click on links or go to pages that don't exist anymore. if a search engine can understand the layout of your site or doesn't believe that the structure make sense or finds all kinds of missing pages, they may not come back as much and they certainly won't be recommending you to other people. Because everyone's websites and objectives are different, there is no bright structure that works for everyone. The most important thing to remember is that your site structure should be apparent to you & it should be obvious to people. Remember search engines are just trying to emulate human processes. So, once you spend some time designing and developing a site structure, this logical and easy for people to understand and navigate through. You can feel confident that search engines will understand your site structure as well.

Recognizing different types of content:

Search Engine Optimization

To understand the different kinds of content that users and search engines can interact with on the web, were going to be taking a look at the http://www.goaholidayhomes.com/ website. One of the most common forms of content on web pages is text content. We see some text here on the Goa Holiday Homes that helps let us know what kind of information we would expect to find on the site. When we click into the various pages we find more text content presented in a few different ways. There are some organize headings and subheadings along with the paragraph, the body text. There's even a check list at the bottom organized by bullet points and when we click on the About Goa, it takes us to a page of content organized by a series of information. All of his different content is formatted in different ways so that is easier for both users and search engines to understand the content. Another form of content found on WebPages is imagery. Images can often be more effective than text in conveying a powerful message.

13 Hotels & Resorts

Hotels and Resorts are great places to spend your vacation and enjoy your holiday in Goa. There are a good range of star hotels with luxurious rooms, delicious on-site dining, relaxing spa treatments and beautiful swimming pools.

23 Guest Houses

Guesthouses in Goa are available in a wide range such as self-catered, bed and breakfast and half board. Our distinctive choice of Goa guesthouses offers quality accommodation at affordable prices for families, budget tourists and couples.

101 Houses For Rent

Holiday rentals in Goa such as Houses, Villas, Apartments, Holiday Homes, Flats, Pent houses, Cottages, Self Catering Homes offer a great experience for your vacation. Find a perfect place to rent in North / South Goa, India and contact the owners directly.

For example on the home page we are immediately drawn to this image of a beach with a beach resorts and it helps me understand the experience of standing on a beach, while the text of this page says the same thing. The feelings and emotions of this message are much better communicated through imagery. Video is another form of content we find in the pages of the web. If we head back to the Video Clips on Goa, we see a featured video clip. The rich sites and video can do what images and text alone cannot. It makes us content really tangible and allows us to almost experience it. There other creative forms of content out there as well: Audio clips interactive animations, recipes and more abound across the Internet. The key is to think about what kind of content will be effective, useful and helpful for your specific audience. The search engines are what may bring visitors to your website. Once they get there you'll need to engage them and ultimately convert them on your business goals and using a mix of the most effective content types is sure to help the user experience.

OPTIMIZING TEXTUAL ELEMENTS:

The main goal of a search engine is to guide people to content that is relevant to a certain keyword or phrase that they searched for. We can fine tune the relevance of your page for a certain topic through the process of on page optimization. The first element was going to optimize is the URL the URL is the location of the page where looking at and you can find it out there in the address bar. You can think of it almost like a file on your computer and much like the path any file on your computer, we can follow some simple guidelines that allow us to create a good URL that can be found and understood quickly. The URL length should be as brief as sensibly likely but at the same time it needs to hold some working information about the page itself. You might find that your website structure uses a system of subfolders and this can be good in that it helps with site structure. Perhaps most importantly you want to make sure that the keyword phrase were targeting is found in the URL. You may go ahead and change this page name. Use hyphens instead of spaces or underscores in the URL. This is important and it helps the search engines to break up words properly.

http://explorecalifornia.org/tours/ backpacking-tours-in-california.html

The next element will look at is the meta-title tag and here were going to go into the source code of a page. One reason for this is at the meta-title tag is also the title it used for the pages search engine result listing. Not only are we trying to optimize the title so that search engines identify the theme of our page.

```
<!DOCTYPE html PUBLIC "-//W3C//DTD XHTML 1.0 Transitional//EN"
"http://www.w3.org/TR/xhtml1/DTD/xhtml1-transitional.dtd">
<html xmlns="http://www.w3.org/1999/xhtml">
<head>
<meta http-equiv="Content-Type" content="text/html; charset=UTF-8" />
<title>Our tour packages</title>
<link href="../css/main.css" rel="stylesheet" type="text/css" />
</head>
<body class="hasCrumbs">
<div id="wrapper">
  <div id="sideNav">
    <ul id="baseNav">
      <li><a href="../tours.htm" title="Explore our tours" class="tours parent">Tours</a></li>
      <ul class="subNav">
        <li><a href="../tours.htm" title="All Tours" class="all">All Tours</a></li>
        <li><a href="../resources/legal.htm" title="Find tours by activity" class="activity">Tours By Activity</a></li>
      </ul>
      <li><a href="../tour_activity.htm" title="Find tours by region" class="region">Tours by Region</a></li>
      <li><a href="../tourfinder.htm" title="Our interactive tour finder" class="finder">Tour Finder</a></li>
    </ul>
    <li><a href="../mission.htm" title="What we think" class="mission">Mission</a></li>
    <li><a href="../contact.htm" title="Contact and support" class="contact">Contact</a></li>
    <li><a href="../resources.htm" title="Guidance and planning" class="resources">Resources</a></li>
    <li><a href="../explorers.htm" title="Join our community" class="explorers">Explorers</a></li>
  </ul>
</div>
```

We also try to entice users to click on it when they see it in the search results. In this example we believe that mentioning the website name might reinforce the context of where this page lives and help convince people to click all result over the others. But don't make the title too long or detract too much from your target keyword phrase. A good rule of thumb is to try to stay under 65 characters. Another meta-tag that we can configure is the Meta Description. Though, optimizing this tag won't get better your search engine rankings & is largely ignored by all the major search engines in their ranking algorithms, it can improve your search engine results click to rate. This is because this tag is often used as the text that shows up under the title of a listing in the search results. You want to spend some time writing compelling text that will lead people to click onto your site and using keywords in your description will help reassure users that this is exactly what they're looking for. Next let's see the H1 header tag. This is normally the markup used for the main noticeable headline of your page and search engines know this. The purpose of using it is to give the reader a apparent idea of what the content is about. You'd have to read through the text to realize that this is actually the name of an organization but most people won't attach around extended adequate to do that and believe about how puzzling that must be to a search engine. There are no defined character limits the headlines; but much like the news world, it's more effective to be concise. Now at this point if you were search engine you've seen a URL a title and a headline that are all talking explicitly about a topic and you're starting to get a pretty good idea of what this page is all about and now we have the content itself. The most important thing about your content is that it needs to be optimized for people first and search engine second. Make sure that your content is written so that it communicates to your target audience in a way that's really engaging. As far as the search engines go there is no magic formula for the perfect page. What you want to remember is that search engines are trying to emulate a human being reading something and then figuring out what it's all about. Search engines are seemed not only for your target keyword but also for disparity of that keyword. Different word orders are also likely to be part of the narrative. Search engines can get very complicated trying to map the semantic & thematic relations among words on a page which is exactly what we as humans do. So ultimately, writing the way that you would write for a human is the best way to optimize for these algorithms and well is no hard and fast rules you might use a general rule of thumb of including your target phrase. One to three times in the text depending upon the length of your content. Don't over believe it and don't overdo it. One last element to optimize on this page is the images. Let's take a look at this first image as person beings, we can glance at this and rapidly form out that those are a number of footprints, but when a search engine looks at it all that seizes a bunch of dots in different colors. It can't inform that they are aligned & colored in such a method to spell out terms or pictures. So they rely on a few other signals to understand what those images really are. Inside this image tag, you can see a few qualities. This tells the browser where to find the image so that it can be loaded. The alt text is reserved for description of the image for those people or browsers that cannot see the image itself. Both of these elements can be optimized to accurately describe what the image is about and also help support the keyword phrase it were trying to optimize for. Just like we change the filename of the page in the URL, we can change the filename of the image and of course rename the image file appropriately to use the keyword phrase were targeting on this page. While there are many more items on a page that can be optimized, focusing on your URL title description, headers body text and images will take care of a very big chunk of your on page optimization. Doing this from the beginning is the ideal situation but take a look at the existing pages of your site after you've done your keyword research and map your pages to your target phrases.

NON-TEXT COMPONENTS:

Search engines are generally very good at analyzing and understanding the text content on web pages. But, they have more difficult time with other forms of content like images videos and audio clips. Let's take a look at a few different ways we can go about optimizing these kinds of content for target keywords. One simple best practice is to use the text surrounding the nontext elements to describe what it's all about. Having a paragraph of text telling a meticulous video right next to the video itself is a very common practice and images embedded in-line with text often have text titles under them and are typically very relevant to the text on the page. Image slideshows or carousels often contain a textual title and description of each photo and an audio clip typically has a report and may even have a total transcription as well. Search engines do examine the text that is in close proximity to the nontext components making the assumption that there is some topical correlation between those elements. The logo is a particular image and even though those pixels are arranged in such a way that humans can quickly read cycle it and see that it's a logo. While the search engine will look at the image filename in the alt text; it will also look at the text nearby and in this case we can see that it's all about telling search engines a little more about that image. Aside from using the text that the near the nontext elements, there's also some code that we can use to help the search engines out. We have already discuss, how we can use the image filename and alt text for an image tag but another way we can optimize code for nontext elements is to use micro-formatting from schema.org. This allows us to markup the code with some very relevant very specific metadata specific to a certain type of content. These are some of the properties that you can define for an image object and their microformat specifications for audio and video clips as well. There is some code that embeds the video and right now there's not much that can tell a search engine about the contents of the video. By adding in some special markup we can provide search engines with all kinds of rich metadata and this will help them really understand what this content is all about. Now when a searcher types in something like Goa Beach, we've positioned ourselves for this page or even this video to pop up in the search results. Take a look through schema.org and you can see all of the different properties and elements that you can define for nontext data. Make sure to provide as much information as you can to the search engines can only help your overall search engine visibility. For video content you can also make use of a video site map file. XML site maps are just files that use a special syntax to provide search engines with a listing of all the pages and content found on your website along with some attributes that describe the content. There are different formats for different types of content and video site maps give us a way to inform search engines exactly where our video content is along with what it's about using things like title and description attributes. Here an example from Google Webmaster tools support and you can find all the specific supported elements and syntax here as well. Using a mix of content types in your pages can be a great way to engage with your visitors and help them down the conversion path and just because a piece of content doesn't use words; doesn't mean we can help a search engine understand just what it's all about. There are surrounding text some code elements and site maps you can open up all of your content to search engines and be well on your way to attracting new traffic to your pages.

CONTENT QUALITY:

For determining just how well that pages but optimized can be difficult to gauge and we may want to isolate more opportunities for improvement. To help us do this going to use the on page report card a tool as part of the SEOmoz Pro toolset. If you're going to get serious about SEO and you want to get SEOmoz Pro account that will give you access to a whole suite of tools designed specifically to help you with search engine optimization.

Let's take a look at the a website. We have already determined that we want this page to be optimized for the phrase backpacking tours and we've taken a look at many of the on page elements that could stand to be optimized in a previous video; but we haven't actually made any changes to this page. Let's run this page through tool to see what recommendations for improvements we can find. We will start by adding or keyword phrase backpacking tours and entering the URL of the page we want to have analyzed that will quickly grade my on page optimization button and let the tool go to work.

As you can see this page isn't very well optimized currently and there are a lot of things we can do. After we get over the initial shock of F graded we can scroll down the page and see that this tool has just provided us with the to do list of all the things that might help this page be more optimized for target keyword phrase. The factors analyzed or grouped by level of importance and we can see that this first section provides us a scorecard of how often or keyword phrase is showing up in various parts of the page. Here are keyword phrase doesn't show up in the title; not in the URL not in the description not in any of our headers, not anywhere in the body or anywhere bolded text or in any of her image alt tags. If you are a search engine, you rank this page for this keyword phrase, probably not. As you scroll down the page you can see additional details about what the tool tested for and whether or not your pages past. You'll also be able to see if the required action is considered an easy, moderate to difficult fix to put in place. If you're looking for a way to quickly generate a fairly comprehensive evaluation of the pages of your site along with a list of recommended actions then, this is the tool for you and following these recommendations to clean up the on page factors of your web pages is the first step to showing the search engines what keywords your content has been optimized for.

USER-GENERATED CONTENT

An important strategy for rising search engine visibility is to repeatedly make new unique and superiority content. But, there is only 24 hours in a day and can be pretty difficult to do that with own resources. Fortunately, you can influence the interest & information of your website visitors to create new content for you and this is better known as user generated content. User generated content is contented that usual website visitors create for your website & known the right circumstances user generated content can be a very scalable and cost-effective means of content creation. So, what are some high-quality examples of user generated content; blog explanation & forums are examples were allowing people to simply express their views can help generate new content. Some websites take this to the next level by taming expert commentary and allowing users to vote or assign weights to certain members of the user community and allowing top contributors and other experts from outside your organization to write a guest blog posts and articles to be a great way to post new and enticing content and have others generate comments and conversations around that content. If you sell products on your site you can allow users to leave reviews of your products as a means to generate new and relevant content. Again you can find ways to organize and display these reviews and you can work on ways to solicit more from your customers. In the business-to-business space you might ask your happy customers to work with you to create testimonials or case studies and keep in mind the content doesn't necessarily need to be textual. If users want to sure interesting information in the form of video clips, photos or other media formats by all means let them. For any form of content that can exist on a website there is the possibility of allowing your website visitors to help create new content and don't forget to take advantage of user generated content through social media outlets. A big reason for the explosive growth of the social media services in recent years is that people have a natural tendency to share interesting content with other people. These services make it easy to do remember sharing content whether you created or your users have provides even greater opportunity for people and search engines to find and see your continent as authoritative. Lastly, you want to make sure that you have some kind of approval process employs if you can let your visitors write or post whatever they want. Unfortunately the world is full of angry people that can and will take full advantage of the ability to post inappropriate things on other people's websites. Make sure to read watch or listen to anything but going up on your pages.

****

CHAPTER: 4
TECHNICAL SEO

The end goal of a search engine when scrolling a page is to try to determine what a webpage looks likes a regular people. But the search engine can't see a page like we do. Instead it sees the code with the Web server some backdoor browsers and to help illustrate this with take a look at a homepage. We see a rich and colorful webpage with lots of content on it pictures, text, menus and videos in all kinds of colors and styles. It's visually appealing and we know how to absorb all this information and how to navigate through it. But a search engine crawler the same page looks like this.

```
<!DOCTYPE html PUBLIC "-//W3C//DTD XHTML 1.0 Transitional//EN"
"http://www.w3.org/TR/xhtml1/DTD/xhtml1-transitional.dtd">
<html xmlns="http://www.w3.org/1999/xhtml">
<head>
<meta http-equiv="Content-Type" content="text/html; charset=UTF-8" />
<title>Come Explore California</title>
<link href="_css/main.css" rel="stylesheet" type="text/css" />
<script type="text/javascript">
    var config = {
        strSelector:"california"
    };
</script>
<script src="/js/cpltc.js" type="text/javascript"></script>
</head>
<body id="home">
<div id="wrapper">
    <div id="mainNav">
        <ul id="homeNav">
            <li><a href="http://explorecalifornia.org/tours.htm" title="Explore our tours" class="tours">Tours</a></li>
            <li><a href="http://explorecalifornia.org/mission.htm" title="What we think" class="mission">Mission</a></li>
            <li><a href="http://explorecalifornia.org/contact.htm" title="Contact and support" class="contact">Contact</a></li>
            <li><a href="http://explorecalifornia.org/resources.htm" title="Guidance and planning" class="resources">Resources</a></li>
            <li><a href="http://explorecalifornia.org/explorers.htm" title="Join our community" class="explorers">Explorers</a></li>
        </ul>
```

Instead, this may not look like the same page we were just looking at. But it is. All of his markup and code are really just a bunch of instructions that are browsers can follow in order to render a great-looking webpage onto our screens. The important part is that this is the code that search engines look at. WebPages are ultimately created with HTML code and markup. This code helps browsers figure out where to find all the files it will need to produce is pretty page where everything is visibly placed in the page; how things are laid out. What font's colors and sizes to use. What side menus will look like? Where links will point to and where content elements are going to be placed? You can see that there's a lot of stuff here in the HTML. It may not end up on the screen and these items provide us with extra opportunities to help search engines understand our content better. HTML is also responsible for loading style sheets which are extra instructions that help define the visible attributes of a page. Front coloring, content sizing, lines spacing, background images, page contents, all kinds of rules for the visual representation of your page can be found here. A HTML is not the only language that browsers can understand. These days' web pages are made more interactive through the use of JavaScript which is additional code that the browser can read and execute and it makes. Things like animation, slideshows and dynamic menus possible. Like style elements, this code can be placed in line or reference from different files. You can also find code that produces different types of nontext content; for example this is a block of code is responsible for rendering the video that we see on the home page. While we as humans can watch the video and hear its message this block of code is all the search engine is able to see. It's important to understand the perspective of the search engine as we go through this book and see what it sees. As you can probably just making sure that your websites code is clean efficient and free from any coding errors will help ensure that your pages are displaying properly to your users. But will also save the search engine some confusion. The cleaner your code the easier it will be

Search Engine Optimization

for you to make adjustments to improve your on page optimization and the more search engines will trust that your pages will be a good experience for your users.

Understanding how search engines index content

It's important to understand how search engines discover new content on the web as well as how they interpret the locations of these pages. One way that search engines identify original contented is by subsequent links. Click through links to go from one page to the next, search engines do the exact same thing to find and index content. Only they click on every link they can find. If you want to make sure that search engines pick up your new content. An easy thing you can do is just make sure you have links pointing to it. Another way for search engines to discover content is from an XML site map and XML site map is really just a listing of your pages content in a special set-up that search engines can simply understand writing. Webmaster can study more about the specific syntax and how to create XML site maps by visiting sitemaps.org. Once you've generated your site maps you can submit them directly to the search engines and this gives you one more way to let them know when you add or change things on your site. Search engines will always try to crawl your links for is much additional content as they can. This is generally a good thing; there are plenty of times that you might have pages up that you don't want search engines to find. Think of test pages for member's only areas of your site that you don't want showing up on the search engine results pages. To control how search engines crawl through your website you can set rules and was called a robots.txt file. This is a file that you or your webmaster can create in the root folder of your site and when search engine see it, they read it and follow the rules of your set. You can set rules that are specific to different browsers and search engine crawlers and you can specify which areas of your website they can and can't see.

This can give it technical and you can learn more about creating robots.txt files rules by visiting robots.txt.org. Again once search engines discover your content, they indexes by URLs. URLs are basically the locations of WebPages on the Internet. It's important that each page on your site as a single unique URL, so that search engines can differentiate that page from all the others and the structure of his URL can also help them understand the structure of your entire website. There are lots of ways that search engines can find your pages and while you can't control how the crawlers actually do their job by creating links and unique and structured URLs for them to follow site maps for them to read and robots.txt files to guide them. You'll be doing everything you can to get your pages in the index as fast as possible.

CANONICAL URLS:

The search engines try to find and index all the pages they find on the net. They rely on single URLs as indicators to each part of content. Even as there should be a single unique URL for each page on the Internet. Often WebPages can introduce slightly varied URLs for the same piece of content resulting in duplicate URLs in the search engine's index. A common reason for this is the use of URL parameters. These are extra bits of data that are added to the end of URLs and may used to do a diversity of dissimilar things. Sometimes they can actually control what content shows up on the page and in those cases the diverse URLs in fact are diverse pages. They could be used for storing session IDs or tracking parameters and will the URL may be different, the content is unaffected. The problem is search engines can't assume which are important URL parameters for content and which are not. One way to resolve this issue on your side is to use the relevant canonical meta-tag this tag is something that you add to your page that acts as an instruction for search engines. It tells them that no matter what URL might be showing up in the address bar make sure to index this URL is the primary URL for this content. Another way to clear up any confusion about how your site uses URL parameters is to tell the search engines directly through Google Webmaster tools and Bing Webmaster tools. Here you can instruct search engines on whether or not they can ignore certain URL parameters. Another reason the duplicate content may exist is because content may have been moved from one location to another on your site. The old location and the new location could potentially be in the search engine's index at the same time and to avoid the situation whenever you move content around it's important to implement redirect rules; there are a few redirect types that you or your webmaster can use, but let's take a look at two in particular the first is known as a 302 or temporary redirect. This should only be used for short-term content moves, like when you want to show that the site is down for maintenance. It tells a search engine that the pages looking for aren't there now will be back very shortly. So please don't do anything to your index. For long-term or permanent content moves which search engines are really concerned with, you want to use a 301 or permanent redirect. These redirects tell search engine that although they may have indexed the previous URL for that content the old URL is no good anymore. The search engine should take everything it knew about the old URL and apply it to the new one, where the content now lives. Ensuring that the search engines know which URLs your pages live on and that you have unique URLs for each of them will help search engines index your pages properly and this is a building block on the path to the top of the search results.

MICRO FORMATS:

Search engines do a good job identifying with the overall content of the web pages about. But you may have parts of the WebPages that contain very specific types of content, like product reviews and embedded video or even a food recipe. Search engines can stand to advantage from a small assist in thoughtful the semantic focal point of these bit of satisfied & fortunately we can give them some assistance. One universal code format that will help us do this is a schema.org microformat. Microformat schemas a special syntax that is use to help search engines identify very specific types of content on your pages. This not only helps search engines identify these pieces of content, it also helps them identify very specific attributes of your content. Here's an example of some recipe text; we can look at this quickly and identify it as a food recipe. For a search engine the short sentences and many line breaks are a bit awkward and they can't possibly understand what each line really means. By augmenting the code behind this recipe text using the schema.org microformat for recipes; you have the opportunity to explicitly tell search engines exactly what this content is. You can see their properties for ingredient prep & cook times and just about something else that you could believe of for recipe. If you think about this from the search engine's perspective, knowing not just that this is definitely a food recipe, but also knowing all this metadata around the recipes will help it to return this content to users that are looking for. If someone is searching for a particular recipes or has an abundance of apples and meet something to do with them the search engines will have a much deeper semantic understanding of what this content through years and they can return it in the search results for an array of relevant search queries. Head over to schema.org and browse the various types of content that have supported microformat, recipes are just one of a lot of. You can use micro-formatting to explain a book with things like author, title, publishing date, the number of pages or you could use micro-formatting to identify an future event by its location, name, dates or even pricing. If you have a brick & mortar business or you're doing e-commerce sales make sure that you're using microformat for your local business contented or your produce contented. As a wide-ranging rule anytime you can specially identify content for search engines you probably should. Explore the different formats to see what may be pertinent for the different types of contented on your site & get started allocation all the great information with the search engines and your visitors alike.

SERVER-SIDE FACTORS

Content and links can affect your websites search engine visibility. Your Web server can also play a big role in how search engines your website. The key here is to make sure that you're serving up pages fast in your serving them up reliably. Remember a search engine is trying to give its users the best experience possible and sending them to a page on the server this down half the time or the takes an eternity to load is not going to be a quality experience. First and foremost a Web server is just a computer and the performance of any computer relies in part on the hardware and the resources it has available. Things like the number and type of processors the amount of memory the quality of the network and the connection to the Internet can all be important. You'll want to talk to the people responsible for hosting and managing your web server to make sure the resources are appropriate to serve pages rapidly & minimize any downtime. The bodily site of your web server can also affect your search engine visibility. As visitors interact with your website, search engines will often collect data around how fast all the elements of your pages are loading for. The visitors in one country in your Web servers located on the other side of the world the page may be loading very slowly which is a concern for search engines. This might seem crazy but it actually happens quite often. Hosting your site halfway across the world might offer financial benefits but also might hurt your ability to quickly serve pages. Generally you want to make sure that your web server is geographically located where most of your potential website visitors will come from. If you expect your visitors to be coming from all over the world, you may want to consider a web hosting solution that can help distribute request for your pages across a global network of computers and even if you're serving up pages locally you may want to consider speeding things up by using content delivery networks or CDN to help serve big files like images and videos from these servers located all over the world. Another thing that will help your pages load quickly is cashing. Your website may be configured to pull content and other information from a database on your web server every time a user requests one of pages. Content management systems like WordPress Drupal Joomla! and more work this way and virtually every product page you've ever seen on an e-commerce site is being constructed from calls to a database. One way to minimize the time-consuming database workload in these situations is to enable server-side caching. This is where your web server interacts with your database only once in order to generate a given page and then it saves a copy of that content on the server for a period of time. Once that copy has been made each subsequent view of that page will load the content that's been saved on the server bypassing any redundant database work. Many content management and e-commerce systems have plug-ins or settings built-in to help you accomplish this. Last but not least you want to make sure that your Web server is consistently running and never experiencing any downtime. If your server is constantly down search engines will consider your site on reliable and they won't want to suggest it to their users. Remember search engines are emulating people and they're trying to reward what we like and analyze what we don't and one thing that people don't like is a slow loading page were server down error message.

WEBMASTER TOOLS:

Let's take a look at how to use the very basics of Google Webmaster tools to learn what information Google has about your website in addition to provide Google with a few orders about how to index. The first step is to go to google.com/webmasters and sign into your account. This requires a Google account. once you're logged in you'll need to submit the domain you want to manage; to protect your account and your website Google will need to verify that you actually own this domain and that you are authorized to see some critical details of this website. There are a few different verification methods you can choose from. But you'll need to do this successfully before continuing. The options that you or your webmaster have include uploading a specific HTML file to your site, adding a specific meta-tag to your source code or making a small change to your sites, DNS record. Another helpful option is the Google analytics access method which you can use if you have Google analytics installed and administrative access to the account. Once you verify the website you'll see a listing for it in your main dashboard. Clicking into this website will bring up a dashboard and a menu of all the different areas of Webmaster tools. You can see some high-level information here around crawl errors and search queries and you can also get a quick view of the number of URLs you've submitted through your site maps and the number of URLs that Google has indexed. You can drill into the crawl error reports to look at what problems Google has had while crawling and indexing your site. Crawl errors can hurt your site and the Google search results so it's important to identify the type of crawl error that's affecting your different URLs and take the appropriate steps to resolve those errors. This may include implementing 301 redirects, or fixing some web server configurations. You may also need to remove references to pages that are no longer part of your site. You can also click on the search queries reports which provide some interesting details about your organic search visibility. You can see impressions as well as how many clicks you got for different keywords and you can also see the average positions your site was ranking and for different keywords over a given period of time. You can also use filters to look at specific search queries, different types of search, different countries or only queries a generated a certain volume of traffic. There are lots of reports and sections of webmaster tools to review and I would encourage you to spend some time going through each for your own website. The configuration section includes general settings like what country your website is targeting, what URL parameters are used on your pages and for what reasons and who else has access to the information in Webmaster tools for your domain. We may looked at the crawl errors report the health section contains additional functionality that lets you block Google from seeing certain pages of your site and also let you know if you've been hacked. You'll also want to check out the optimization section this is where you'll be able to review and submit your XML site maps as well as take a look at the HTML improvement section to identify potential problems with your sites content that you can address immediately. As you can see there are many other features to Google Webmaster tools that you should explore and there are always more new features coming out .Google has done a very good job of letting you know how it views your pages and allowing you to provide input into what it knows about you. Staying on top of Google Webmaster tools month after month is certainly an endeavor that will pay dividends.

BING WEBMASTER TOOLS

Google isn't the only search engine out there with tools and another one that you want to get familiar with his Bing Webmaster tools. Much like Google Webmaster tools this will allow you to learn what information Bing has about the pages of your site and it will

Search Engine Optimization

give you a chance to provide Bing with a few instructions about how to index your website. You'll need to have an account with Bing and once you're logged in you'll need to submit a domain to gain access. When adding a site still have two quick options: first you can provide the URL to your XML site map, if you've got it and if you don't worry you can always do this later. You can also select what time of day your site gets the most traffic and if you do Bing will try to crawl your site during off-peak times. Your next step is to verify that you own and control is website. You can do this by clicking the verify now link from the sites page that you see when you first login. In order to prove that you control this domain you can choose between uploading a specific file to your Web server, copying and pasting a meta-tag into your default page or making a small change to your sites DNS record. Once you verify the website, you can click into it and you'll see a dashboard containing statistics that can give you an idea of your search visibility for clicks and impressions over time as well as any recent crawling and indexing trends.

Scrolling down, you can view overviews of the search keywords and inbound links reports and clicking to see all links will take you into the full reports. The search keywords report shows clicks and impressions for each keyword as well as average rankings and click through rates over a given period of time. The inbound links report displays a graph showing the count of inbound links to your pages that Bing knows about overtime and you can click into any of your pages to see who's linking to them. another important report is the crawl information report which you can find on the left-hand menu under reports and data; here you can identify any crawl errors that Bing is found and if you see any it's important to implement fixes for those errors you'll also notice data for any redirects that you have on your website so that you can ensure that your content moves are being handled appropriately. While you should certainly take a look at the other reports in the reports and data section, it's also important to make sure that your providing Bing with whatever information you can about your site and this is done in the configure my site section.

Here you can manage your XML site maps configure any URL parameter rules that will help bring understand your URLs, control how Bing crawls your site, and tell it what pages allowed to see. Last don't forget to explore the diagnostics and tool section where you'll find a host of tools to help you further optimize your site. Keyword research tool works in much the same way as Google's and can be a great way to find even more keyword ideas. Just make sure to remember that the numbers you're seeing are from the Bing search engine so you won't want to compare these with the Google tool. You should also take some time to play with the SEO analyzer tool. This works quite a bit like the SEOmoz on page report card providing you information about any errors or issues you can fix for the page. Only this one does not take into account the specific keyword like the SEOmoz told us. Although Bing's share of the search market is certainly much smaller than Google's, it's still a very sizable group of people that you can afford to ignore and not only do Bing's Webmaster tools give you the ability to optimize your Bing presents as best you can. They can also provide a richer data set in an alternative point of you for your overall SEO strategy.

****

CHAPTER: 5
LONG TERM PLANNING

With many businesses turning to online as a medium to market their products and services, it's more important than ever the business owners understand why having a content strategy will help push them forward and achieve success with the research objectives. A content strategy is the planning, creation and management of working content. Let's take a look at each of these workings independently. Writing content and posting it or syndicating across the web, you need to have a plan. This start by understanding who your target audience is and what their needs are. Think about content as bait in your audience with the fish. If you use the wrong kind of bait or if you throw the right bait and upon were there are many fish that's no good. You won't catch what you're looking for. But understanding who your audience is, where they hang out and converse online and what they are talking about will assist you to both find goals & learn what's significant to them. When you couple this with keyword research you have a strong understanding of the themes and the kinds of topics that you want to produce content for. When it comes time for the actual creation, there is no question that content is king. Creating content is a task that you're going to need to factor into your online marketing plan, whether you like it or not. If you're not writing content and publishing on the web, you're losing out on a share of traffic to your site. Every way that you can think up to help your potential customers that's relevant to the themes and keywords that you've targeted in the audience that you're going after is an opportunity; and if you think about it if you're not answering the common questions of your customers are asking then your competitors will. Content creation involves writing usable, relevant and targeted content. The quantity of content is not nearly as important as developing quality pieces the customers can always refer back to and share with her networks. For SEO purposes, remember that it's the content that attracts audiences and links and relevant high quality pages are then rewarded further with authority in the eyes of the search engines. Whether it's you, your team or outsourced help is responsible for executing on this plan, you'll need to make sure the content is being written on a regular basis for the keywords and audiences that your targeting and once your content is been created, it needs to be managed and maintained properly as well. A sound content management system with team members write, edit, post and maintain content quickly and efficiently helping with workflow and encouraging a more collaborative environment that each member of the team can be a part of. Going through the cycles of planning, creating and managing usable content will have you well on your way to executing a sustainable and successful content strategy.

CONTENT STRATEGY:

Every organization is different. We all operate in different environments and we all have different goals. So everyone's ideal contented plan will be single; but what content policy work and which don't we can look at some of the core components of content strategies that successful organizations share. The first is clearly defined your goals and objectives. Knowing what keywords you researched and chosen to target what your audiences are looking for and ultimately what you want them to do when they get to your site is the foundation of everything that will do. These goals will help you with reporting and measurement and put a realistic perspective on the fallout you achieve. You can achieve lots of goals e-commerce sale to more leads and phone calls to more followers on social networks. Goals can be anything but they should tieback to your bottom line through business objectives. Second spend the time to really understand your key audiences and their needs. Perhaps the cornerstone of a good content strategy is to research your audience and then understand them well enough to be able to market to them effectively. Knowing your customers role in an organization, location, the demographics, their interests and their behaviors will help you step into their shoes and bring insights into the planning process. Third, is ensuring that everyone in your organization is involved. This isn't something that you're going to be able to talk alone and you'll need buy-in from your CEO all the way down your interest. If your smaller organization, you might even consider outsourcing some of the work once you found the people involved group is one that's passionate and excited to spread knowledge. Getting the people in your organization on board is not an easy thing. But having a plan with a good thorough reasoning and clear expectations around your goals can help persuade them to jump on board. Forth you need to ensure that everyone in the organization maintains a healthy respect for online reputation management. Whenever you put anything out there on the web it's there forever and as they are standing by your brand. You can't un-tweet something and if you publish something in error odds, some server somewhere has already captured and stored whatever it was that you didn't want up there. Many businesses today have well-crafted and well-thought-out policies for writing and publishing content on behalf of the company. But many still don't. If you fall in the latter bucket, you want to invest some time to define just what people can and can't post and what editorial procedures need to be followed. Always remember that anyone on the web can read and find your content when it goes live. Ultimately your reputation will dictate whether customers want to do business with you or not. The last thing successful organizations do with the content strategies is spending time monitoring trends. The only thing that's certain about the Internet is of the online marketing landscape is constantly changing. New competitors are popping up by the minute. all competitors are doing new things your business environment is changing faster than ever before. In your target audience is changing along with. What this means is that what works for you today won't necessarily work for you tomorrow and you have to embrace the fact that this is a moving target that requires your full attention if you want to stay ahead. monitoring trends involves not only keeping a pulse on your industries, but also things like renewing keyword research and reviewing your content structure and strategy a regular basis. Maintaining industry relationships having continuous contact with influencers and industry leaders to get the inside scoop and finding new and creative ways to relay those messages to your followers. While successful organizations tend to exemplify these traits this isn't by any means a complete list. Take a look at your own organization your own objectives and then define your own success.

DEFINING AUDIENCE:

Defining and understanding your target audience is the first step for writing content for them. Attracting just anyone to your website isn't so hard. It's drawing the true kind of people and contributing the correct topic in the right tone and style; it's a challenge. A good way to start is to simply ask the question for the people that who do we want people visiting our site and what goals with a plan organization. From here, we can go through the exercise of understanding how they're using online channels and where we might be able to message were engage them. A great tool to start off with is the Forrester Text-and-Graphics profile tool.

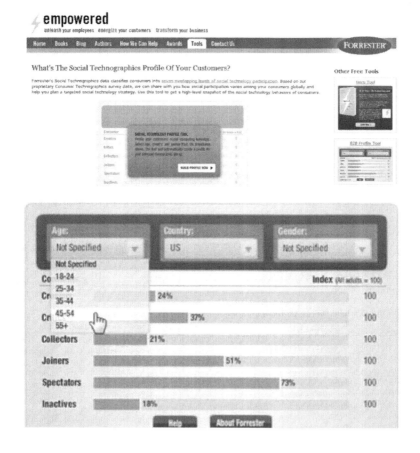

Search Engine Optimization

This tool can help provide insight into how your and consumer uses different technologies today. For example, if we were targeting a group of US males between the ages of 45 and 54, we can see that the majority of them are what we call spectators. This means that they often spend their time on blogs, videos, podcasts, forums and reviews; but their reading and not necessarily contributing. Knowingness we might tailor our content to these formats and we know will need to work harder to get any user generated content from these folks. Once we know what kinds of content our target audiences consuming and we've identified who they are, will need to drive in and look at our topics. Ultimately users are typing keywords into search engines and keywords remain the core and foundation of SEO. So when it comes to choosing topics want to tie them to the keywords were chosen based on relevance, search volume and competition during or keyword research process. You also want to look at tools like Google trends for search to monitor industry trends and understand what popular among your target audience and what's being searched for and discussed. Matching your topics to what's popular and being searched for will maximize the size of the potential audience for your catering to. Next you can employ the concept of filling in the gaps. Odds are good that someone else already wrote something about your topic; and the last thing the Internet needs is more pages talking about the same old thing; instead figure out what's missing out there and fill in those holes. Monitor what your competitors are writing about. But more importantly monitor what they're not writing about. These are great opportunities for you to offer unique perspectives and even more value. Once we've identified who were writing for and what were writing about the last thing we need to do is define our content angles. This is really nothing more than the approach to writing your content and it should be consistent, appropriate to the audience writing technical articles for rocket scientist to read or lighthearted commentaries on the state of the entertainment industry. They have very different tones for each and above all remember that while we're doing all this to support our business objectives and ultimately some kind of sales, no one wants to read a blatant sales pitch. We need to offer up something of real value; content is compelling and useful to the reader. When you're deciding how to angle and position your content you want to consider a couple more areas of importance. First the original whenever you write take the time to make sure that it's unique and that it comes from your own voice. You want to bring something new to the table that will excite your readers that they can't find anywhere else. Whether you decide to be humorous or put a creative twist to your content, it needs to keep him engaged or even entertain from beginning. To end when they're done reading it they should be thinking I now know something interesting that I didn't know before; or even better still be thinking I need to share that with my friends. From a format perspective you'll want to think about the style of content that you're putting together. You will you be writing a blog post or informative style articles are you taking a comparative style where you contrast product A with product B without discussing a before and after scenario or a how to walk through and remember the content isn't just text. Pictures are worth 1000 words and you can; even use video to capture sights and sounds to convey complex concepts or to make something more tangible to user. By understanding who your writing for, what you're writing about and what style your writing in you'll be cementing the foundations of thought full unique and relevant content that will both human readers and search engines alike.

DIFFERENT CONTENT TYPES

You might think the content is just text on a page. But these days it is not the case. Content can take many forms; including presentations, images, info graphics and even video. Lots of

Search Engine Optimization

content out there are in textual format. These are the words we read on pages blog posts, articles more and as we've seen the text we choose and how it relates to the keywords we want to target with our SEO strategy is extremely important. But, don't forget about other file formats; PDF files were documents and even presentation slides are all forms of content, we interact with day in and day out and they can all be published on the web. You can usually bring the content from document formats into an HTML format for the web; many people don't think about the presentations. If you have a slide deck that you recently presented 10 posted on the web and share with the audience after the gathering. More speakers & companies are manufacturing a custom of uploading the slides to slide hosting services like slide share before they even give a talk. They can provide a link to the deck that can be downloaded so that audience member can go after along on their laptops and share the presentation with others.

This can provide a catalyst for sharing from content that you've already created.

Using images can be a great way to tell a story visually or to help readers envision exactly what the text on a pages describing and images are quickly evolving as their own kind of content all across the web. Think of the popularity of sites like printerest but are completely driven by groups of images & commented by people all over the world & search engines are indexing image content too. Head over to Google.com and search for your company or brand name in Google image search? Does it return the results that you expect? While users expect images to be part of the online experience and you can help search engines, understand pictures as part of a page with the correct code. Image search convey a new way of penetrating for and noticed content in and of it. Another popular piece of content that is popped up is the infographic.

Infographics represent a concept or a large set of data in a visual way and they can help people absorb and distill a lot of information in a meaningful way that can quickly be understood. Infographics are typically just image files and are often found on pages with plenty of context around them; so they can certainly be indexed and searched on in search engines and well designed and constructed infographics on popular topics have the added benefit of getting shared around and reference from other sources. These days video is everywhere and not only do most of us have high-speed data connections to our computers. We also have them for phones and tablets too. Video production is never been more economical and telling a story with sight and sound can help you get across the message that text and images simply convey and remember that the video content can be optimized for search engines. By syndicating your video through popular services & correctly selecting your video title and categories as you do, you can position your videos to be found in search and don't forget to transcribe your videos into text that can be used for closed captioning subtitles and that search engines can read. YouTube is one of the most popular video hosting services out there and it allows users to upload and share videos online for free. It also happens to be a Google property and you've likely seen YouTube videos showing up in search results. If you're producing video content that at the very least you'll want to make sure to get yourself a YouTube channel and post your videos there. Filling in all the metadata that can help your content show up when your potential customers are searching. It is important to keep in mind that text is not your only option, different audiences will consume different types of content and search engines are capable of indexing & returning all kinds of things. knowing what types of satisfied are out there will not only help you think more strategically about what to publish but it will also keep you on your toes and above the competition.

GETTING IDEAS FOR CONTENT

Getting ideas for writing content can be tough and many people struggle of the stage of the game. Only you can figure out what content will accomplish your search engine optimization goals. There are a few things you can do to get the creative juices flowing. First, think of your website in terms of some very broad themes; then think of the different ways you might be able to present those things. Content can be classified in many ways and thinking about the style you could write it, may shake some ideas loose and started on a path. Educational pieces can be used to show your users how to do something or to teach them something that they didn't know before. You could take a statistic fact or figure from your industry and expand upon it offering value from the perspective of an expert opinion. You can get technical and focus on details or advanced topics that appeal to confidence users or other industry experts. Procedural content can be a step-by-step how-two type of article that walks the visitor through a certain process. Informational content doesn't have to be groundbreaking or prize-winning; just putting up a page of driving directions to your store or biographies of your key executive team or both content opportunities that may be missing from your pages. News is simply an informational page that references something that happened at a specific moment in time. This could be industry newsletter. Reporting or commenting on or it could be company news about who you hire or a recap of the conference that you just hosted. All of these can be applied to a broad array of themes and there are certainly many more not included in this list. It might help to have your target keywords in front of you as you run through this list. The combination of specific phrases and types of content can often be the source of a great idea. The second thing you can do as a source of inspiration is scan your competitors to see if you're missing something or if there is a whole lot there that you can fill. Do a quick search on some of your keywords and click on some of your competitors. You can spend some time on the sites and take a look at their blogs with their FAQ sections. What kinds of things with writing about other categories that you can offer new unique insights into other hot topics that you can expand upon or burning questions that you can answer. You can also take a look at your competition and social media. With a tweet and posting about maybe they got the industry's group if you missed. That might be something right for a commentary piece. Third the people you work with each and every day can be hidden sources of fantastic content. Customers are often happy to leave reviews and provide feedback if you asked them to a mirror lots of ways that you can ask. Calling up or having a face-to-face conversation with your best customers can lead to a case study or testimonial that you can put up on your site that shows real customers having good experiences. For search engine that can represent both good content and authority. You might ask a customer to do a full review of one of your products or services for posting on your website or run a contest were customers write about their experiences for a chance to win a sweepstakes or prize of some kind and don't stop with your customers. As an organization you have a network of people that you work with. This could all provide some kind of content for you. Call up your vendors and asked them to write a joint case study that you can publish on your website. If your peers give you an award or an industry partner gives you a certification, you can be creating content around and don't be afraid to reach out to your professional networks. Your industry contacts might just be willing to offer a guest blog post if you asked them. Coming up with content ideas can be hard. Remember that means it's hard for your competitors too. Looking at the kind of content pieces you can write taking stock of your competitors in your industry and leveraging the people you touch day-to-day can help you come up with the content that might just attract your next customer.

EDITORIAL CALENDAR

An editorial calendar is perhaps one of the most important parts of your content strategy and without proper planning you'll find it difficult to establish consistency or structure in the content you posting to your site. An editorial calendar simply maps out your content development process assigning writers and dates to the topics of pages, posts or other content that will be going up on your pages. Here's an example of an editorial calendar and while you can certainly use this format to get started.

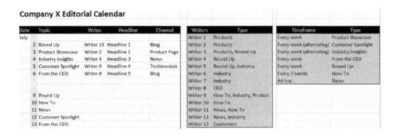

Keep in mind that there is no single editorial calendar that will fit every business. You want to update this to the format and structure that you're comfortable working with them that fit the unique needs of your content strategy. First let's take a look over to the right hand side of the spreadsheet where we define the different content types that we want to build content around: things like product showcases, new stories, how-to articles and things of that nature. Yours will certainly be different but listing them out here along with the approximate frequency with which you'd like to publish this kind of content will be helpful columns. H and I list out the different writers that we can pull from along with the types of content that their willing and able to write. You might be lucky enough to have a team of copywriters that you can call upon. But if not keep in mind that these folks can is anyone working with you. You may require your sales team to write one piece of content per month your management agrees to put together one blog post every two months. Whatever resources you have to help with content, listing them out here will help you see who's available to write what when. The left-hand side of the spreadsheet includes a row for every day of the month, listing what days specific content is due, who's responsible for and where on the site will be published. In this case we can see that there's new content going up on this site five days a week spread out over a company blog, news pages, product pages and a customer testimonial section. You can see the column is reserved for the headline of the content that's going to be written. In many editorial calendars will go so far as to list the target keyword title and descriptions as well. Again feel free to use his format as a template for creating your own editorial calendar. But make sure to add in whatever you feel is necessary for your own organization. And although this one has been done in Excel it's often a good practice to do this in Google spreadsheets, so that the document can be shared across your team and everyone can collaborate on the same document without having to pass around different versions of the same file. You also need to define how often your planning will happen and how far out you'll be making assignments. Some organizations work week by week. Whatever you choose, you'll need to make sure that writers are given sufficient time to produce high-quality output. They are not writing just for the sake of putting more pages on your website. Remember that quality wins over quantity. In the end and editorial calendar will only be as useful as the person taking charge of it and the people taking action from it. building out a plan assigning authors and topics and holding people accountable for delivering will ensure that your consistently putting up good content and don't forget to promote the content as well. Many organizations include their social media and promotion plans right inside the editorial calendar indicating who will be sharing what on each channel what hashtags will be used and who is responsible for keeping conversations going. Using an editorial calendar to keep track of your content strategy can be a great way to put the structure around this process which is needed for consistency.

SOCIAL MEDIA

Social media can be a great way to let the world know your content's out there and can even be a source of referral traffic in its own right helping potential customers find you. But social media is still pretty new and many businesses have jumped into it without really knowing how to use it effectively. The first thing you'll need to do if you want to leverage social media to help get your content out there is to make sure that your company has a presence on at least the top social media networks. We are talking about the ones with the largest number of active users Twitter, Facebook, LinkedIn, Google+, YouTube. Every one of these networks is a chance to get your content in front of more eyeballs. Attract more links and encourage more sharing. Once you've established a presence on these networks you want to make sure that they are integrated on the pages that host the content you're creating. Lots of companies maintain a blog with an RSS feed because it's a great way to get the word out to qualified visitors. They are actively subscribing to your content. You can do a similar thing with social media by placing the various share buttons on your pages and these allow users to quickly pass on content they found useful to their own networks that said you want to choose your social share buttons careful. You don't fill your pages with 20 different buttons that took to have days to load. You want to pick the ones that your audiences are active on. For example if you've got a strong presence on Twitter and Google plus. Make sure you put the Twitter and Google plus buttons on your pages. If you're trying to grow your Facebook or LinkedIn following, placing those buttons there might be a good idea as well. But if you don't have a MySpace or orkut page, you don't target users of those social networks you may want leave them off and make it simpler for your consumer base to make their selection. Keep in mind also that many of these share buttons are configurable; for example you could optimize the default twitte to include your Twitter username to encourage recipients of that week to follow you. On Facebook you can control which image thumbnails to use as a default. As you build and grow your presence on social networks you'll find topics that you relate to that are guiding conversations in the social sphere. On Twitter and Google plus hashtags are commonly used to tag certain conversations and people that are interested in those topics can choose to listen to tweets are posts that contain specific hashtags. You can find existing hashtags by searching keywords on Twitter about your industry or by following influencers who tweet regularly and seeing which hashtags they use. For example the web analytics community uses the # measure in their tweets. Many of the expert's converse and share interesting content with one another using this #. Your are creating content that fits the bill you can use that # to get your content in front of a very specific group of people. Remember though this is a self-regulating community. Your content must be useful and valuable to that group and if it is you'll be rewarded with further shares and retweets. A good thing to do when planning your content strategy is to identify how you plan to share that content across your social network once it's been pushed live and which networks will go out on. What will the message said? what hashtags will use? Respond to the activity and keep the conversations going. These are all questions to keep in mind with each piece of content that you publish. Last, the popular social media outlets of today are not likely to remain constant forever. Remember friends to MySpace about Netscape and AOL in this industry company's rise and fall faster than ever before and you'll need to keep an eye on the networks that matter for your audience and respond to them accordingly. Whichever networks you choose and however you choose to leverage them spending the time to get the word out about the content that you worked so hard to create will be well worth the effort.

CONTENT PERFORMANCE

Measuring the performance of your content is essential to determining the success of your SEO efforts and to help guide your content strategy. By looking at how your content performs, you'll be able to understand what your visitors want and provide more of it to them in the future. When you evaluate your content performance it's important to ask these questions. What content are visitors looking at. What our most popular content or are visitors engaged with our content or are visitors sharing our content with others and is our content generating quality business results. If you haven't already you can install a free tool like Google analytics to collect data you'll need to help you get the answers to these questions. First figuring out what our customers are looking up can be measured by simple page views and Google analytics you can head over to the content reports and you'll see a list of the most popular pages of your website for the date range are looking at. If you want to find out which were your most popular pages as landing pages or the first page a visitor sees when they come to your site, you can head over to the landing pages report. If you are an advanced user, you can even use custom segments to look at only visits that came from organic search or even specific search engines and well it's good to know which pieces of content got the most page views that doesn't tell us anything about how well the content was received. Writing content is easy for writing content that will provide value and leave an impression on your visitors is much more difficult and that's where were interested in finding out about visitor engagement. There are three metrics that can help you quickly tell how well visitors are engaging with your content: pages per visit, average time on site and bounce rate. Visitors are considered more engaged the longer each of their visits to your website is and this can be measured by both average time on site and the number of pages they viewed during their visit. The bounce rate is a measure of how often a visitor lands on your website and then leaves without seeing any other page of the site. Generally speaking the bounce rate, the more your visitors were enticed by your content to dive deeper into your site. Next let's look at whether or not our content is being shared online while you can use a slew of social media tools to measure how often your tweets and posts, pluses and shares our research throughout your social networks. Tools like Google analytics can also be configured to track interactions that are happening both on and off your site. Google analytics can track how many times people are clicking your social media sharing buttons or leaving comments on your blog and it can even go out and find the public posts across a number of different social networks that have been used to share content from your site. Of course the flip side of this is that when content is shared via social media the recipients of those tweets and posts can come and visit your website. You can use campaign tagging and Google analytics traffic sources reports to see how many of your visits are coming from all the sharing. Perhaps the most important question of all is whether or not all of his content production is driving our business goals. Properly configured, web analytics tool is focused not just on counting pages but associating all of that data with business outcomes. To the visitors who came to your site as a result of particular piece of content end up buying something, calling us, that they submit a leave form or download a white paper, sign-up for a product. Each and every one of these goals as a real business value and by understanding what content drives these conversion actions; we can answer the biggest question of all. What did we get back for our investment in SEO whether you use Google analytics or any other analytics tool monitoring and measuring the performance of your content will help you understand the value your creative and help you plan for and continually improve the content you'll be focusing on next.

****

CHAPTER: 6
LINK-BUILDING STRATEGIES

One of the most important aspects of SEO's links and this has traditionally been the backbone of how search engines work. As search engine crawl all the pages in the world, they find the links pointing to other pages. You know that blue underlined text that you see everywhere that you can click on in your browser takes you to some other page. You can think of each one of those links is a vote and not every vote is the same. Remember that some sites are considered more authoritative and more trustworthy than others. In this way to democracy, there are really just two things that matter. The number of links you have pointing to you and the quality of those links. Generally speaking you improve your search engine visibility by increasing your link popularity. The more quality links you have pointing to your website from other websites the more authoritative your site will be to search engines. If no other website was linking to yours. It would be very difficult for search engines to trust your site enough to return it in the search results. A search engine would much rather show results from sites that have earned links and authority. But you can have all the links in the world and it won't matter unless those links are of high quality. One thing search engines look for to determine when quality is how relevant the link is to the content on the pages. For example, if you run a recipe website and you end up with a food blog linking to you the search engine has no trouble at all with that relationship. It makes perfect sense of the food blog would link to a recipe website. But if you went out and told your friend who owns a gambling websites to put a link on their site over to yours that's can be a little harder to justify. A gambling site probably has no business linking to your recipes and since that the connection isn't there. A search engine may not place as much value on that link. Search engines will also look at the link text itself the text that you can click on is what's known as the anchor text and if you think about it that anchor text serves as a pretty good clue as to what the destination page is all about. A search engine doesn't even need to go to the page and it already knows what to expect. Think about that compared to a link that uses anchor text like link or click here. Unless the page is really about links were clicking here, it's not going to tell search engine much about what's on the page. Another indicator of quality is freshness and trends. Search engines expect you to naturally gain a steady amount of links over time and if you don't, it might be interpreted as a bad thing. For example if a bunch of links to your site showed up on the Internet five years ago and you had nothing since then, your content may be considered stale and your site would be less authoritative and less trustworthy. On the other hand, if you've never had anyone link to you in your life and then on one certain date, there was a pattern of 100 new links showing up on random blogs on the same day every single month, the search engines are going to investigate a little deeper and they might find out that you hired someone to buy you a bunch of links every month and while we're talking about spam this is probably a good time to say that it is highly recommended that you not try to trick the system. Search engines are very aware of just about every technique out there and there are some very real penalties for getting caught trying to manipulate the system. If a search engine finds an extremely large amount of similar links with the same anchor text popping up all over the place or links that appear to have been paid for or suspicious groups of websites known to practice spamming techniques or any number of other factors, it's very easy for them to figure out exactly what you been doing and then penalize you for. Penalties can be anything from dropping your rankings for minor infractions to dropping you from the entire index if you're doing really over things. Remember search engine optimization is not something you do for short-term gains. It's something you build upon day after day to build long-term value. Finally we've entered into an era where social media is now part of our online lives. When people post ensure links to your content or indicate its quality by clicking a button, search engines are taking note. If you think about or used to have to rely on other websites in the way to democracy, social media allows of a signal that actually tells them what people like. Understanding your audience and the keywords are typing into search engines and creating great content around it is the first step to SEO. But earning the links back to your website around the web is what really shows search engines just how trustworthy and authoritative you really are.

INTERNAL LINKS

Earning links back to from people and websites, you don't control is a necessary but challenging thing to do, but don't forget about the links you do have complete control over. Determining how you link to pages on your own site is important for search engines as well. Internal linking help search engines understand the structure of your website, the topics and themes of your content and even the relative importance of each page has on your site. We can break down internal linking into two different types: of navigation links and contextual links. Navigation links are typically links found on the top side or bottom of your web pages. You can think of them as part of the framework of your site. Navigation links are present on every page of the site and there used to help guide users as they click around your site and find what they're looking for. Search engines will analyze your navigation links to determine a hierarchy of pages that drill down from your homepage and will be able to see how your content is organized and how flat or deep your site structure is. Outside the navigational framework of your website, you'll have contextual links. These are links within the content of a specific page, that point to another page on your site and just like external links these can be very helpful when the content of one page makes reference to the content of another page. Contextual links help users by cross-referencing other relevant information; but they help search engines too. Search engines can look at the anchor text of an internal link to help it understand the content of the page the link points to. An internal links help the search engines determine topical relevancy between pages and the importance of a page by the quantity of internal links pointing to it. When you're building your website, make sure to give some thought and planning to the navigational elements you plan to use across all of your pages and when you're writing content, make sure you're taking advantage of linking to other pages on your site with contextual links that use appropriate anchor text. Both your users and the search engines will appreciate it.

EXTERNAL LINKS

Building quality links to your website will improve its overall popularity in the eyes of the search engines and improve your search engine visibility. But you're probably thinking what most people are thinking at this point. How I get links pointing back to my site when I don't have control over other websites out there. The good news is that links come in different forms and can be generated from different tactics. First there are some easy ones. A very common way of generating links is to submit your website or business to different web directories. But keep in mind you're going to want to be extremely selective about the directories you submit to. What you don't want to do is click on one of those absences will submit your website to 4 billion search engines and directories for a dollar 99. There are lots of spamming directories out there and there are very few that are actually trustworthy. A good guideline to follow is whether or not the directory conducts some form of editorial process that reviews each link and only exception relevant and trusted websites themselves. If a directory is willing to publish any link without any review it's probably not a reliable directory. The Yahoo directory is a good place to start and if you run a local business, you can submit your information to the different search engines respective local business directories. If you have industry-specific directories and listings services that are trusted and you need to your market, those are good places to go next. Another way of building links is to entice other websites to link to your content and the key factor here is that you need to have quality content; the people are willing to link to. In a search engines perfect world, someone reads a piece of content and says wow that is so fantastic that I have to link to it and sometimes great content attracts links naturally as a result of people discovering it and sharing it around. But there are other times when you may have to do a little outreach to get people to discover your content in the first place. Leveraging your social connections to share the fact that you've posted new content can get the word out and don't stop there. Try to find other websites that you feel have the same audience; for example there may be a professor at a university is doing research in your field and publishes her own blog about topics that are very relevant to yours. Reaching out to the professor and letting them know that you have content that their own readers would find interesting and useful, might just earn you a very relevant and very trustworthy link and beyond generating links

Search Engine Optimization

from other websites, these days, it's crucial to gain links from social media sharing. People are social beings and were very eager to share content we find interesting with our friends, our families and our colleagues. To search engines this is a fantastic signal that tell them what content people actually like and what real people are actually interested in. So use those sharing buttons on your content pages and use your own social influence on the networks you participated in to get links to your content out there and passed around. Keep in mind there are some very bad ways to build links too and you can be penalized for doing this wrong way, so be careful. As a general rule, if it feels like you're trying to cheat the system, don't do it. Getting caught is something that will inevitably happen and when it does there are some very real consequences that are not easy to undo. Imagine trying to run your business without anyone ever finding on a search engine. Another rule of thumb is that if it's too easy, it's probably going to get you in trouble. Don't fall prey to the companies out there offering to sell you 1000 text links every single month or post whatever you want them to on their blog for $20. Don't trade links with perfect strangers that have absolutely no relevance to your business or your content and don't put yourself on listings are directories that exist solely to get you more links. As with most things common sense will keep you out of trouble. The web is constantly changing and evolving in the search engines are too will allow this change with the search engines over the years. The importance of links has remained intact and that's because quality and insightful content will always attract readers willing to share your content. As long as your link building tactics, keep those key elements in mind you'll always have an opportunity to build new quality links.

LINK-BUILDING OPPORTUNITIES

Search engines reliable links to determine whether your web pages are trustworthy and authoritative and to earn and uphold that status, it's important to always be on the lookout for new link building opportunities that you can take advantage of. One simple way to find new opportunities is to analyze the back links of other websites ranking for a target keyword phrase. The logic here is pretty straightforward; if a webpage is ranking well for the keywords you're targeting they must have some good back links. By examining their links we might find some that we like to go after as well to help out our own rankings. Let's take an example and say we want to find new link building opportunities for the phrase backpacking tours. The first thing to do is head over to Google and do a search for that term. The top results are ranking high in part because of their on page optimization. But another strong reason they write so well is because they have a lot of good links pointing to those pages. What we want to do is analyze who is linking to those pages; determine how they got those links and create a link outreach strategy to emulate those efforts. One tool we can use for back like research is Open Site Explorer, another tool that part of the SEOmoz tools . Let's pick one of those top ranking URLs from the previous search and enter them.

Search Engine Optimization

You'll see lots of information about this page. But the first tab labeled inbound links list all the pages linking to the one where examining. You can play with all the various filters to narrow down this list according to different criteria. But for now were going to show links from only external sources. This means we are not going to list links coming from somewhere else on the same site. You can examine each of these links and your goal here is to gain an understanding of whether or not the link would be a good fit for you and if so what will be your link outreach strategy. One thing to remember is that you want to build strong quality links to your own site. So try to focus on back links with a high page authority or a domain authority. You want to be on the lookout for a few different kinds of opportunities as you go through these lists and one thing you may discover are additional directories that you can submit your site too. You should have already submitted your site to many high quality directories. But there's a good chance that you've missed some and this type of analysis will let you see what other directories your competitors have discovered that maybe able to help you as well. Another common strategy that may uncover opportunities you can take advantage of is guest blogging. This is when you reach out to another website and offered to produce content for their blog. This can be a wind-win arrangement with a blog it's content that helps their site and their users and in return you include back links to your site within the content that you've produced. Not only does this help with back link development, but it can also strengthen your industry relationships provide an outlet for thought leadership and improve your status in your industry. You also want to be on the lookout for links from nonprofit sites. Many companies will support nonprofit organizations through donations, expertise or in-kind work and many times these organizations will link back to your site wherever they may highlight the sponsors and organizations that work with. Links from these domains are generally considered very trustworthy by the search engines. So you might want to think about what causes are important to your organization and consider supporting them or reach out to the nonprofit you are already working with and see if there's an opportunity for a link or story that can be published on their site. Another great method is to produce high quality educational content to post on your website for the specific purpose of garnering a link back to it. There are many sites in just about every industry vertical was primary purpose is to promote industry-specific education and guide their users to informative content. By creating high quality informative content that fills gaps or by creating relationships with these sites to understand what content they are in need of you'll gain a network of people and pages that are happy to link to you. Once again this is a win-win situation with a third-party site, gets the benefit of directing their readers to trustworthy content and you get the benefit of gaining links from trustworthy and relevant sites. There are many more strategies that can be uncovered from competitor back link analysis and the key is to spend time analyzing what opportunities are out there and how you can take advantage of them.

LINK-BUILDING STRATEGY

Executing a link building plan requires organization during your outreach efforts as well as a way to monitor the progress of building new links over time. One tool that can be really helpful in managing your link building prospects is Raven tools.

Search Engine Optimization

Raven tools has a lot of features to help you with your overall Internet marketing efforts. But one that's particularly useful is the link manager. The link manager tool helps you manage your outreach efforts allowing you to track your progress from the moment you decide you want to try to get a particular link until well after it's been up and found by the search engines. You can assign the status of the outreach what kind of linkages and who in your organization has a responsibility for this link. You can enter the website you're reaching out to and you can also add the URL and anchor text of any links you generate, which the tool monitor over time providing uptime status and went value reporting. You can also enter the contact information of the person you're working with to gain this particular link and you can add any additional details around the process, conversations you had, an overall progress report in the description tab. As you start identifying link opportunities and building relationships with the different people out there that can help you turn them into realities, you might find that you are juggling a lot at any given time. Using a tool like raven to keep track of everything with tidy, sort able and filterable lists can really help keep this process organized and on track. As you gain links over time, the other thing you want to determine is whether or not these links are increasing the overall authority of your site. One tool you can use to get a current snapshot of the value of your current links is the open site Explorer tool from SEOmoz. Just enter any one of your URLs and you'll be able to see a numeric representation of both the domains authority as well as the specific page of typed in. To get some rich historical background data, you can use the back links history feature from yet another tool called majestic SEO. This will give you some insightful trend graphs to let you know how strong your link outreach is performing over periods of time and looking at the cumulative view it can help you see how you're progressing. You can even compare yourself to up to four of your competitors to see what they're up to and how you stack up. Being organized in your outreach efforts and having access to link performance information will give you control over your efforts and data to measure how you're doing over time. Having these tools and processes in place is a key part of maintaining the ongoing forward momentum that you need to keep building high-quality links.

CHAPTER 7
EFFICIENCY OF SEO

One of the biggest challenges you might find is in figuring out whether your SEO campaigns are succeeding or failing. SEO measurement not only involves the analysis of basic metrics like traffic, resulting from organic search engines and specific keywords. But it also requires a holistic approach to measuring business outcomes and making adjustments based on data. If you've never paid attention to SEO before, there are some basic things you'll need to have checked off your list. Before you can do anything, you need to make sure that you have an analytic solution installed. Something like Google analytics, Adobe Omniture site catalyst webtrends or coremetrics will do the job. You want to invest some time and resources into making sure that your web analytics tracking is implemented and configured properly and recording data accurately. This means that you'll probably need to go beyond slapping some JavaScript on your pages and at a minimum you need to configure your analytic solution to track goals and business outcomes. But the sky is a limit on what you can track these days. Ensuring a robust and complete implementation will make your day to trustworthy enough that you can use it to make confident evidence-based decisions. Once you collecting the data you need to define your business objectives and the key performance indicators or KPI's you used to measure them. For example you might want people to submit a contact form on your website. That case, you can configure your analytic solution to track that is a conversion action and you might look at KPI's like the number of conversions that occur and the conversion rate. This is just one example, remember you'll have lots of goals for your website and that means you have lots of KPI's to continually monitor and improve upon. You also want to establish some SEO specific APIs that can help you understand how your SEO efforts are paying off. Things like organic search traffic or visits to your website from search engines that are not generated by paid search but organic listing. Your total organic search traffic compared to a previous timeframe like month over month or year-over-year. No branded keyword searches or searches were your brand or your business name was not part of the search term and target keyword rankings or how well you rank for each of your target keywords. While this last one might not be available in your standard analytics reports, there are plenty of tools out there that can automate the monitoring of keyword rankings over time. Anyone working in a sealed that's worth your paycheck should be keeping an eye on these metrics of the minimum. This is really just scratching the surface. While attracting traffic to your website through your SEO program is certainly important. You also need to see what the traffic is actually doing once they get your site. When you analyze traffic that comes from a certain search engine, as a result of a certain keyword search and lands on a certain landing page, you should also start to look at how that traffic converts on your business goals. If you're an e-commerce situation than you should obviously be looking at things like revenue, average order volumes and other transactional data. But even if you don't sell your products online you still got lots of things to track. you can look at reads a come in the form of newsletter subscribers, social followers event or demonstration sign-ups driving directions to your brick-and-mortar store, contact forms or anything else you can dream up and these days there are lots of analytics solutions allow you to track phone calls back to the source of traffic as well. Make sure that you're measuring all of these important business goals so that you can look at the conversions and conversion rates from the traffic your SEO is generating. Ensuring that you're collecting the right data, reporting on your KPI's in a meaningful way and analyzing the data to really understand what's happening with your SEO strategy is a foundation. But, just looking at the data doesn't change anything. Measuring and improving your SEO over time is a continuous cycle of measurement, learning and taking action. You have to use the data to learn what changes you can make your strategy and once you've made those changes you'll start the cycle over again by measuring whether or not those changes produced an improvement. Until you reach perfection there's always something you can be doing better. In a data-driven measurement plan for your SEO will have you on the path to continuous improvement.

ANALYZING KEYWORDS

Keywords are the backbone of search engine optimization and when were measuring our SEO efforts, analyzing the different keywords that are bringing people to our websites is an excellent place to start. Inside Google analytics we can navigate to the organic search traffic report by drilling down through traffic sources, sources, search organic.

this report will show us all the keywords that have driven traffic to our pages from organic search engines and although were only looking at 10 by default, you can change this to show up to 500 rows at a time. Another quick tip is to use the secondary dimension drop-down, so that we can see which search engine sent us the traffic. Just select source from the drop-down and you'll see another column of data show up with this information. By default will be looking at general site usage metrics and here will be able to get some insights around just how engage visitors are that find our site through certain keywords. If you haven't yet configured goals in your Google analytics account to track business outcomes make that your top priority. You can't manage what you can't measure and that goes for all of your online marketing efforts; not just SEO. Once you got your goal set up you can click on a goal set to see how your keywords are performing with respect to your business objectives. Of course if you configured e-commerce and Google analytics you can also look at not just goal data but transactional data for each of the keywords you're analyzing. One thing we need to mention is that in late 2011, Google made a change to how it allows web analytics tools to capture keyword data from organic searches. If a user does a search while logged into their Google account, Google now encrypts the keyword data so that it cannot be read by analytics tools and unfortunately this means that all of those keywords are dumped into a generic role of data called not provided. Here we can see that over half of the organic traffic to this website came from users that were logged

Search Engine Optimization

into Google and unfortunately that means that the keywords that they used are unavailable to us in Google analytics or any other web analytics software. One thing that we can do is drill down on that not provided link and change your primary dimension to the landing page. This will at the very least allow us some insights into how the ranking pages are performing and if we combine this with data around which of our pages are ranking for which terms, we can often in for the keywords that led to these visits. Remember that when you're looking at keyword reports, you're only seeing data for people who found your website the research that you ranked for and they clicked on you in the search results. What that means is that web analytics is not a very good indicator of what opportunities you're missing. If you don't rank for a keyword no one is going to be clicking on a search result for you and no data for those missed opportunities will ever show up here. Make sure to continually look at data from your keyword research tools as well to identify keyword opportunities and once you do start getting traffic from them, you'll be able to analyze how they perform in your web analytics tools. One thing you can do is link your Google Webmaster tools account to your Google analytics account. Once you've done this you can view all of this data under traffic sources search engine optimization. In the Google Webmaster tools queries report, you can find data on impressions and search engine results, your average right positions and clicks and click through rates. Note that these numbers are perfect so feel free to take the data in Google Webmaster tools reports with a grain of salt. That said it's still accurate enough to get some valuable insights based on the trends rather than the raw numbers. One thing to look are keywords that have high impressions but low click through rates. This means that you might be showing up in the search results but no one clicking on your listing. This could mean that you've got problems with your title or maybe your description and it's worthwhile to take a closer look. With all of the data available analyzing keywords can be an intimidating task but it's an extremely important one for anyone doing SEO; because everything begins with the search understanding what happens after searchers click on those pages that we worked so hard to rank for is the key to putting a value on all of our efforts.

ANALYZING LINKS

Over time, if you are consistently putting out good quality content, promoting it and working through link outreach opportunities, other websites will start linking too. Being able to clearly see what's happening to your link portfolio can tell you how you're doing in your quest to show the search engines just how trustworthy and authoritative your website is. There are two exceptional tools for analyzing back link metrics: Open Site Explorer by SEOmaz and Majestic SEO. you can use these tools to analyze links for any website; not just your own and looking at your competitors back links can be a great way to discover new link opportunities. When you're analyzing your own back links however, we want to take a look at some metrics that can tell you how your link building efforts are going. Using Open Site Explorer, you can produce a report on domain and page metrics for any URL and you'll also see a list of the pages that link back to that website. Along the top we have different metrics that tell us various things about. We can also see the total number of links coming into a page as well as the unique number of domains that these links are coming from. You can see some public social metrics as well. Though they have some limitations based on how this data is collected. We really looking to do here is make a habit of checking in on these numbers over time and our goal here is continual improvement. The higher your site's domain authority the stronger and more able your domain is to influence rankings and as your link portfolio grows, you should expect to see your authority scores rising as well. By filtering down to just the back links coming from external pages, you can look through each of the links that you have coming back to site and identify any areas for action. For example you might find that a blogger that you have a relationship has a link to you. But you like them to use different anchor text and that link that reflects a keyword that you need some help with. You might also find opportunities for guest authorship or you may find links that you don't want to be a part of. In any of these situations knowing who is linking to you and how can help you manage and expand your link building efforts. If you want to automate the process of monitoring domain, page and link metrics you can do this using SEOmaz as campaign tracking feature. Once you've created a campaign within the tool, you can navigate to the history report in the link analysis section. You'll be able to see how your site compares with the websites you've added is competitors over a period of time. You will see graphs for things like domain authority total number of links and specific types of links that can help you gauge how your link building efforts are going. There's lots more data and reports you can explore within the tools of SEOmaz, but let's switch over to majestic SEO now and look at the back links history reports. The back links history shows you the number of links you acquired on either a monthly, cumulative or normalized basis and you can use it to get a sense of how your link portfolio has grown, since your website launched. You can also define up to four other competitors to compare yourself against and this can help you see how you stacking up to the sites if you're trying to beat out in the search results. The two sections you'll see are the back links discovery graph which provides the total number of links out there pointing to your website and the referring domains discovery graph which let's you know how many different domains have links pointing to your site. By consistently growing your link portfolio you're building a strong trust with search engines and as a result your pages will be better positioned to rank higher in the search results. Using tools like these to help manage this process can provide feedback as to how your efforts are working and keep you on the right track as you continue to move forward.

Analyzing the impact of social media

SEO experts in the industry have been testing social shares and how search engines may be handling the signals in their algorithms to rank pages for quite a while now and Google's stated what most SEO's now believe. They do you social signals to determine rankings. Let's take a look at a few ways to measure how your content is being shared and identify the most shareable content on your website because social sharing has an impact on your rankings, it's important to look at what's worked in the past so that we can make improvements in the future. There are lots of tools out there to measure and manage social media these days, but one you should take a look at his cold Social Crawlytics. You can use this tool to audit your pages and see how many shares from a variety of social channels are pointing to your site. Social Crawlytics covers eight social media channels: Facebook, Twitter delicious LinkedIn, Stumble Upon, Digg, Google plus an printerest. To start you can log in with your Twitter account and you'll just need to enter a website address in the dashboard screen to initiate the crawling process. Depending on how deep your site structure goes you may need to adjust the crawl depth from 2 to 3 or four. This tool only crawl HTML content pages so keep in mind that, if you have other types of files on your site this will be discarded from the report. When you're ready click submit and the tool will start crawling and processing the results for your domain. It may take up to 10 minutes for your report to finish. The completed report will appear in the reports tab and you'll find a page filled with figures and charts. The summary tells us how many times your websites pages were shared up to the depth you specified for the crawl. The page shares per network bar chart breaks down all the pages crawl and shows you which channels were most active. In this kind of information helps us understand where we have a strong presence we can take advantage of as well as which networks we might want to work on. Hovering over any of the slices of data will show us the actual content that was shared on that channel. Further down the page you'll find a table with the results listed by page URL. Having this data to look at as you continue to create and promote content on your pages can help you determine how useful and shareable your content is. By analyzing what kinds of pages tend to get shared and how effective your promotion strategies are, you'll be able to ensure that your offering the right kind of content and promoting it in a way that will get out there in the social networks for both people and search engines to find.

****

CHAPTER: 8
ECOMMERCE

These days lots of people use search engines for shopping whether in the early stages of research or the ready to buy something right now. Whatever stage of the buying process therein, if you sell the products are searching for, your going to want to be found and there are a few different things to consider three specific e-commerce websites that can help search engines match your pages to the intensive people search queries. First and foremost remember that everything that applies to normal content also applies to e-commerce pages. The common best practices around website linking structures, external links and on page optimization or all very important. but in an era where search engines want to explicitly identify content at the most granular level of detail that they, can we want to make sure that search engines are very clear that your e-commerce content is exactly that. Beyond the typical HTML code that is found on web pages you can use very specific metadata to help identify your content as e-commerce content and describe the products of your offering. But even before you put in place those technical components, it's still as important as ever to know what keywords your potential customers are typing into search engines. Make sure to analyze your keyword research to determine what intent, people have when using certain keywords and what content are looking for. If you find the people are searching for comparisons between you and your competitors, then you might consider building content specific to that meet. For those typing in keywords that indicate that they are further down the purchasing process like buy product X or product Y coupon. You want to ensure that the content you're creating contains an easy path to the shopping cart. One more thing that unique need to e-commerce is at the products that you sell are often been discussed outside the bounds of your own website. You can find discussions on forums social media or other websites about the products you sell and these can be opportunities to jump into the conversation as a knowledgeable product expert. If someone is posting a review of their experience with you, you can use things like Google alerts or social media monitoring tools to make sure you're aware of it and good about it's an opportunity for you to listen and join the conversation. If people are expressing negative feelings about you or your product, you can reach out to them and resolve the situation in the public eye. If people are saying good things about your products reach out and say thank you. It might even lead to social media activity that ends of building links or user generated content for you. All of these public mediums are seen by search engines as well as people and you can gain some very tangible benefits from both.

SEMANTIC HTML:

E-commerce sites are different for most normal websites, because they are very specific content about very specific products. To help search engines identify the specific parts of content we are going to take advantage of micro-formatting from schema.org. Schema.org contains many schemas that can help identify different kinds of content and that includes e-commerce content. Your e-commerce site will have product pages and these pages should be using the schema for products that founded schema.org/product. In your code you can specify a product name, description, product image and even brand manufacturer and model information. Another element you can associate with your products or offers. Offers have a whole list of properties that you can populate; things like how much are selling a product for, the availability of the product what the condition of our product is or what date the price is valid until. You can also markup any rating information that you have for a product by using the rating schema. This can be found at schema.org/aggregate rating and to take further advantage of user generated content you can apply micro-formatting to the reviews you are collecting on your products. Schema.org/review provides syntax run properties like the title of the review who wrote it, when it was published and of course the content of the review itself. If you operate a local business as well as an e-commerce storefront you can also provide detailed information about your business locations. You can use micro-formats to specify your business address along with a link to a map, the contact information for that location and a description of your business. If you have more than one location, make sure you're doing this for each one individually and you can even associate reviews photos and events with each of your listings and make sure to take a look at the schemas that exist for specific types of businesses; like restaurants and professional services to see if there's elements are properties that make sense for you. Taking full advantage of the schema.org micro-formats for your e-commerce specific data is a great way to make sure that search engines know exactly how to interpret your content and investigating the various micro-formats are out there might help you out more relevant content that you wouldn't have otherwise thought of.

Search Engine Optimization

TECHNICAL COMPONENTS:

E-commerce websites are unique and other constantly evolving because of product inventory that's coming and going. These websites tend to be very large as well which can increase the chances of technical issues being introduced. If you're running an e-commerce site, there are some specific things to watch out for and some things to put on your to do list. First if you're out of stock or product, the product changes slightly or you're not selling at the moment but you expect to at some point in the future, make sure to leave the page intact but of course update the page with the appropriate messaging. You don't want to have to start from scratch especially if you're already getting good traction with the search engines. But if a product no longer exists in any form, make sure that that product URL returns a page not found with a status code of 404. You should make sure that your 404 page has been customized to provide an appropriate message letting users know that you're sorry that they didn't find what they're looking for. You also want to include navigation, search bar or perhaps even some suggested phrases so that anyone that lands here as a way to continue shopping on your website. If the product page location is just moved like that was assigned to a different category, you want to make sure to implement a 301 permanent redirect to take users to the right place and to let search engines know that this is the new home for this particular product. With content that's always changing, we also want to make sure that the search engines have a way to discover your new content right away. Make sure your e-commerce platform generates an XML site map of your entire website URLs. Most e-commerce platforms can dynamically create these XML site maps as your site changes from the same database that drives website itself and many of them can submit the site map URLs to the search engine webmaster tools as well. Making sure this process is in place ensures that search engines will always discover your new content right away and don't forget to place the relevant canonical tag on each of your pages. This will make sure that search engines are indexing only unique URLs for each of your category, subcategory and product pages and it will ensure that you don't run into any duplicate content issues. Again many e-commerce platforms will do this for you or offered is a feature that you can enable and configure. Last a common presentation style on e-commerce sites includes paginated content. For example, you might have 30 products in a particular category but there displayed ten per page. To a search engine this might look like three different pages. And it can be confusing to search engine crawlers as they traverse your website. Fortunately you can use the realm next or previous attributes on your pagination links to tell search engines not to treat the link page is a unique page but instead is just an extension of the current page. Keeping in mind the extra technical components of an e-commerce website will help search engines to clearly index your content and understand the products you offer. Setting you up for a better chance of being returned when users come searching.

ECOMMERCE INFORMATION:

Just like any other kind of website, search engines need to understand how your e-commerce content is organized. With a well-organized structure, your content pages e-commerce specific pages and even the products themselves will be clearly recognizable and identifiable to search engines as they crawl the pages of your site. Remember the internal linking is crucial for helping search engines understand the structure of your website. When you walk into a store in the off-line world it is organized into different sections to help visitors have the right direction before they actually start looking for specific products on the shelves. Websites should be built with the same concept in mind using your linking to set up that structure. At the highest level of your hierarchy, you can identify the different categories of products of you sell and within those category pages you can link to the next level of subcategories are products. By doing this search engines will be able to understand what it is you sell and what categories your products fall under. This allows him to return the best most relevant pages of your site to searchers. If someone will search for shoes. For example a search engine can return your general shoes category page. When they start searching for a certain type of shoes then you want them to end up on your subcategory page for that particular type of shoe and if there typing and model numbers and specific products, you want the appropriate product pages being returned. We get to the actual product pages themselves, there are a few things to remember. First each and every product should have its own unique page and on each of those pages you'll need to include content around the product. That means including things like the product name, properly tagged images, robust and unique product descriptions, product colors, sizes and other options, prices whether or not it's in stock and a host of other attributes we typically associate with e-commerce products. Over and above the page content we even have the ability to identify those attributes even more clearly to the search engines by adding special metadata to your code. And of course don't forget to make sure that you are including your category, subcategory and product pages in your XML site maps. You can even wait the relative importance of each tier of pages or specific pages themselves to give the search engines an idea of which pages you feel are the most important on your site. The more you can help search engines with identifying the details of your e-commerce product information, through your site structure, internal links and metadata, the more they will trust your site with providing a quality shopping experience for users and all other things equal, the more likely they are to return your pages over the competition.

ECOMMERCE CONTENT:

Creating content for e-commerce sites serves a number of different purposes. First it needs to be attractive to the search engines so that people find your pages. once you've got people on your pages, the content needs to be effective not only in encouraging people to buy your products, but also in getting them so excited that they want to share your content with other people through links and social media which helps your overall SEO. One thing to simply describe a product, but people are a little more complex than that. Going back to marketing 101, we don't sell products and services, we sell solutions to people's problems; so make sure to describe more than just a product. Describe how the product is actually used and take opportunities through photos, videos, animations or even step-by-step diagrams to really show your customers how this thing works and how it will solve the problem with are having. This is something your competition is probably not doing a great job of and it will give you an angle on some very unique content that will stand out to both search engines and website visitors alike. You also need to remember that your visitors are aware that if they buy something from, you used and benefit. It's like when you going to the electronic store and the sales person is on commission recommends the most expensive camera. You know that it's because will make the most money, if you buy that one but on the web we have the option of reading to reviews from people just like us were at that same crossroads and ended up making the decision to purchase this product. Now were going to tell us what they think about that decision and they're not getting a commission. As consumers, we tend to trust these reviews and displaying product reviews or service testimonials is a great way to help people understand the value of your products through other people's experiences and last don't forget to include additional product recommendations. If your e-commerce software have this built-in, make sure you're leveraging it and if not, take a look at the many product recommendation engines out there on the market. As people browse certain products you can recommend other similar products of people tend to buy that have great reviews or that match other criteria. and this can be a great option for cross sells as well. If someone puts that Camera are shopping cart, you can suggest of the give some lenses a carrying case and an extra battery as well. Taking the time to create comprehensive and unique product pages that help users solve their problems; re-assure them through other people's experiences and help them through the conversion funnel will benefit you not only in your sales but also in the search engine visibility.

LINK BUILDING FOR ECOMMERCE:

Building links and getting people to your e-commerce content can be challenging but with a little creativity you can find some very valuable opportunities that will help out the search engines as well as your visitors. First and foremost, make sure that your taking the time to create really good content. Anything you can do to help show how a product will solve the problems of the consumer is going to be a good thing and it becomes a lot more shareable than just another product name and description page; over and above videos and diagrams and things like that, there are a few ways to spruce up your product pages even more. With a little work, some out-of-the-box thinking and a good programmer, you can come up with interactive features that can help the customer really understand your product. Think of those clothing websites that allow you to put together an entire wardrobe through a drag-and drop interface or home decor stores that allow you to layout and generate your dream kitchen or living room. Whatever you are selling these kinds of useful features are the kinds of things the people blog about, link to and share with their social networks. Another thing to remember is that investing in high quality images of the products are selling is something that will pay off in the long run. Blogs and image-based social networks are filled with users willing to share quality, beautiful and interesting images associated with your products. Take time to produce and promote professional, high quality, unique images and you'll be in a good position to garner even more links back to your content and at the end of the day don't forget about your customers and remember that they love a good deal. Free stuff giveaways, discounts and special offers are the kinds of things it gets shared around the Internet and can spread like wildfire. You might feature a section on your site that shows your current deals and coupons or you might run a contest or sweepstakes or even have a crazy deal of the day page that offers up a loss leader, but gets people talking about you. You might break even or even lose a bit on your promotion. But think of it as investing in all the links to blogger attention in the social media buzz that will find your new customers and that search engines love. Last don't forget to let your users generate some content for you. Whether it is product reviews that you ask for in follow-up emails after a purchase, testimonials or social media integrations, making it easy for your users to share their experiences leads a lots of potential links sharing and user generated content that can help future customers, make the decision to buy from you instead of your competition. While adding a standard social media sharing and liking buttons your product pages is a must. You might also think about providing save to my wish list or share with a friend functionality that can spread the word and keep people coming back. In short doesn't be another boring e-commerce site with boring product pages. There are plenty of those out there already. Instead go that extra mile to produce truly useful and engaging content that excites your users and has the potential to gain links and social media shares. Get creative; take time to think about your audience and what can be really useful to them and then take the time to create the right effective content that meets those needs.

INTERNATIONAL AUDIENCES:

If your target audience crosses countries and languages, there are a few things you want to do to help position yourself well for the search engines. First and maybe the most obvious, you'll want to consider having your content translated and regionalized for the market you targeting. This can be a big investment, in you'll need to do this right which means you're not going to get away with dumping your site into Google translate and copying and pasting back in your e-commerce platform. But the investment is going to pay off for you, because people from different countries that speak different languages are going to be typing in different keywords and the search engines are much more likely to return relevant and quality content that matches a user's language. The next thing to do is to have a unique URL for each of the translated versions of your pages. Many e-commerce solutions don't do this. So you want to check and make sure that as you switch between languages; the full URL in the address bar is unique for each. This allows search engines to separate one paid from another when determining relevancy for search queries and visitors using different languages. And don't worry about translated pages being considered duplicate content by search engines. Although these pages may be talking about the exact same things search engines are very good at distinguishing languages and treat different translations on separate pages as different pieces of content. From a technical standpoint, we can help search engines identify what language and country the content is targeted to by providing specific metadata on a pages. We do this with what's called the Hreflang link element. Say, we have one version of a page in English and one version of the page in Spanish, we can use these two link tags on both pages to let the search engines know that these are translations of the same page in specific languages and we can get even more specific. For example, if we had a special version of the page that was translated into Spanish and regionalized to Mexico, we could instead use a link tag that specifies both the language of Spanish and the country of Mexico. Crossing borders and languages can be a challenging and rewarding experience and making sure that your pages are optimized for the regions and languages you're targeting will help you attract and convert the right audiences.

CHAPTER: 9
LOCAL SEARCH

If your brick-and-mortar business or if you have a local presence than it's important that you know it's a fact. Your potential customers are using search engines to look for local products and services and search engines are doing pretty good at giving users exactly what they want, with some very specific local types of search results. Let's say you are in Delhi with a toothache need some immediate attention. These days the first thing you're likely to do is head to a search engine and start typing dentist Delhi and looking at the current market share data, you're more likely to do it on Google than anywhere else. In the search results, you'll see a list of businesses in the Delhi area matching your search. You'll see some special listings with location markers and a map that shows you where all those businesses are located. When you click on that marker, you end up in a Google maps interface showing a map of the area surrounding the business and plenty of information and reviews on the left. for each business listing that you see, you can either click the link to the website or head over to that particular businesses Google plus local page or you can find reviews photos and even see you who when your social circles has anything to say about the business. The bottom line is that if you're a dentist in Delhi and you don't have this kind of local listing on the search engines, your phone isn't very likely to be ringing. So how do you position yourself to have your business featured in the special local search results when people type in search queries with a local intent. There are a few things that you can do. First, you're going to need to have a Google plus local page. If you're not on Google plus yet, now is a good time to start and you can walk through the process of setting up a Google plus account and a Google plus local page for your business. If you how to Google places account it's already been migrated to Google plus local for you and you can simply login and make any updates or changes to leverage the new format and don't forget to ask your happy customers for reviews on your Google plus page. The more reviews and a more positive they are, more likely Google is to return your pages about the competition. Next, you need to understand the concept of citations. Each and every mention of search engines find around the web of the name address or phone number of your business is considered a citation and the more citations a business gets from quality sources, the more the search engines trust that this is a business searchers are looking for and the higher it can rank in local search results. Next your website is a critical piece of your local marketing strategy. You want to make sure that you have separate pages on your website for each service or category of products that you offer and you want to make sure that your business is name address and phone number are clearly identified on your website. Of course remember your content strategy and make sure that you have relevant keywords in your copy to ensure optimal search performance. Focusing on creating, maintaining and growing your Google plus local page, building consistent and quality citations of your name, address and phone number around the web and focusing on the content of your website of the key ingredients that you'll need for local search success.

Google+ Local:

Search Engine Optimization

Google plus local, which used to be Google places is a place where businesses can get themselves a robust and feature-rich online listing for free. When you create a business listing on Google plus local, you'll have the opportunity to provide basic information about your business, photos and more. Users will be able to leave reviews for you in. As an administrator will also get to see statistics about your visitors and the searches that they've done to bring them to your page. But all this is only going to be seen, if your visitors can find the page and there are essentially three factors that influence rankings on Google plus local: Relevance, distance and prominence. Relevance is all about how well your business listing matches a user search term. In most cases, the more complete and accurate a business listing, is the easier it is for Google to properly understand your business and return its listing in the search result. Also, more relevant your businesses to the search term, the more relevant as to the searcher, which is more likely to provide the quality experience of the search engines want and get you to click. The second factor is distance; local searches are by definition bound to a geographic location and Google uses knows about where a searcher is physically located including location terms in the search query. It then attempts to return the most relevant results based on listings in specific area. In many cases, larger metropolitan areas are divided into smaller parts. So you'll need to consider how you choose to list your business and Google plus local; for example, cities like Delhi, Mumbai and Kolkata are all considered part of a broader Indian metro area. But, if you live in any of those places you wouldn't be searching for a businesses using Delhi in your search word. As a business owner you want to think about how local be typing in their queries and mimic that is best you can. If you have multiple locations, you should create separate listings for each to maximize your exposure on the search results and make sure that your closest location is the one that the user sees. Finally the prominence of the listing has an effect on how well we rank. Prominence is a measure of how well known your businesses across the web and much like regular content pages, it looks for evidence around the web that others are talking about you. Things like links, reviews, articles, blogs directory listings and any other mentions about your business or all considered and generally, more positive these mentions of your business are the better. To maximize your chances of ranking well in local search results, just remember these three things: make sure that your listing is as complete, accurate and relevant to your local searches as possible. Make sure that you define your distance from searchers by defining the exact area or areas that your business serves and just like you do with your general SEO strategy; work on building your brand, customer relationships and loyalty to earn prominence around the web.

Optimizing Google+ Local:

You'll need to list your business on Google plus local sort can appear in Google local search results. In the first step is to visit www.google.com/places for business. Before you login here's a tip; when signing up for Google plus local, it's a good idea to create separate Google accounts to manage your listings. In this account should really be tied to your corporate domain; something like local@yourdomain.com. To keep your business account tied to the business and separate from your personal account. If you and the organization you're working for ever decide to part ways, the separation can save you a lot of headaches later on. Once you've logged in for the first time you'll be prompted to enter your phone number and Google will tell you if it already knows about your business. If it does it will pre-fill whatever information it's found on the form will need to fill out. This is your chance to provide as much information as you possibly can to Google about your business. So you want to fill out all the required fields and as many optional ones as you possibly can. You'll start off by entering your

Search Engine Optimization

company name in the company organization field. It's important that you don't try to add keywords to your company name to get a higher rank. Remember that consistency across your citations is extremely important to local search rankings. So this can actually hurt you and it's against the terms of service. Since consistency in your name address and phone number is so critical, sometimes it can be helpful to ensure that there is a default but you're using everywhere you can. One trick is to write up a business name address and phone number just once in a text file and then store that text file somewhere that anyone doing this kind of work can access and when you're updating citations, you can just copy and paste the information from the document. This will minimize the chances of the information being inconsistent or incorrect. Next, fill in the email address that you want associated with your business and your website. Although these are optional, it's a good idea to use them and you can take advantage of the 200 character description of your business. You want to think about your target keywords, but ultimately this should be enticing marketing copy that describes what your business does and why consumers should choose you over the competition. The next step is choosing the categories under which are going to list your business. Category suggestions will appear as you begin typing and you want to choose one of the suggested categories if you can. You can also use the add another category link to select up to five categories. The service areas and location settings section, asks whether your customers come to you or you build your customers; for example if you're running a coffee shop chances are your customers are coming to you. Wedding photographers on the other hand usually travel out to their clients. You can also enter your operating hours and the payment options that you accept. Generally, you want to provide as much information as you can throughout your listing. Remember potential customers are searching on the go and if they know for a fact that you are open at a particular time or except the credit card that they have in their wallet that might be enough to bring them into your door, instead of your competitors. Photos and videos are a great way for you to showcase your business to potential customers and really show them exactly what though be getting if they choose to do business with you. If you are running restaurant, pictures of tempting plates of food friendly service send a great atmosphere might win you a new customer. You might even put up a video of your salad bar or a walk around the dining room. Whatever your business an additional 10 images or five videos to your profile can help someone decide whether to come in or stay away. The last piece of the puzzle is the additional details field and this is where you can get creative. If you have anything else to say about your business this is where you'll put it and will Google plus local won't display this section in your listing, it's still worth your while to add as many details about what makes your business unique as you can. After you fill out the form you'll need to verify your business listing before it will go live. Google plus local will send you a pin verification code either by mail at your business address or by phone and once you receive your pin you need to enter it into your Google plus local account to verify that you actually do own the business you've claimed. Once your listing is online, you can always come back to edit or add photos videos or anything else that hasn't already been added to the listing. The more you tell Google about your business the easier it will be for the search engine to understand what your business is about in place you appropriately in the search results. The more detail you provide in your listing the better chance you have of convincing customers to walk through your doors.

GETTING MORE CITATIONS

Having accurate information on the web is extremely important. If your information is incorrect, it can hurt the chances of people will find you and that's not good for you or the customer that you could have served. The more a search engine can trust your location information, the more confident it can be in returning your pages to the local search and for these reason citations are extremely important. A citation is any mention of your business name address and phone number on the web and this combination of information is often referred to as nap for short. Aside from having as many as possible on quality sites, citations should also be exactly the same wherever they appear. You can check how your business looks on lots of directory website by visiting getlisted.org. Getlisted is a site that provides information on local search and you can use the tool to find out how well your business is listed online by entering your business's name and ZIP Code. Get listed will then look up the listing across a host of different popular directories and give you a listing score that tells you how well you've use the free listings, search engines used to collect local search data. Clicking on each of the tabs to the left will provide even more information on the accuracy of your business information reviews and other things you can do to improve your listings online. For example, in the accuracy tab you'll see your business information listed on a number of local directory websites. Here we can see that the Google listings still needs to be claimed.

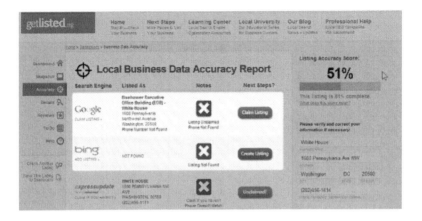

In the bidding listing doesn't even exist and we can also see that there are some differences between the name, address and phone number among some of these listing sites. You can also see that there are slightly different phone numbers that are shown across different directories. Having this information is crucial and by claiming each of these listings you can make the changes to the information to ensure that the name address and phone number is consistent across the mall. Another great part of get listed other studies of local citation sources for each city and category found in the learning center area. These will tell you which local citation sources are the most popular in each city and for each business category and they can be very helpful in finding specific listing sites that you'll want a citation from and when you run out of things to discover on get listed, there are still lots of places that you can list your business and it's just a matter of digging a bit deeper to uncover them. A great tool for this is the white spark location citation Finder tool. Here, you can research and manage all of your local citations in one place. You can search by either key phrase or phone number. In the search results you can scroll down and get a list of lots of potential citation sources you may want to go after. If you find citations that you already own, you can mark them as got it. You can also mark citations which don't make sense for your business as useless. These options can help you organize your citations in a meaningful way and help you keep track of which ones you're getting over time without wasting hours looking at the same websites over and over. The quantity and quality and consistency of the citations that search engines find around the web for your business are an important factor in how well you rank in local search and having tools like these to manager existing citations and help you find opportunities for new ones can make a big difference in your overall local search strategy.

REVIEWS

Online reviews can be a major asset for businesses and this is especially true for local search. Recent studies have shown that for a majority of consumer's positive reviews build them more possible to use a local commerce and that the trust these review as much as personal recommendations. If you're not getting reviews online, you are missing out on a huge opportunity. Reviews not only assist you build a reputation, they can also bring more customers to your front door. Review is a short write up or rating provided by customer based on their experience with a particular business. Reviews can be found on search engines, local review websites and services or even blogs. There are basically three ways a user can provide a review of your business: off-line, email, website. Many businesses communicate with their customers every day through phone calls, physical mail, or in-store interactions. Every one of these off-line flashpoints is an opportunity to ask customers what they thought of their experience and you can use negative feedback to help you improve your business and turn the positive feedback in the testimonials that can be used on your website or promotional materials. If you're still not collecting email addresses on your website for visitors that want to subscribe more about you, you're missing out on a huge marketing opportunity. Creating maintaining and growing a list of your customers and those were actively interested in becoming your customers, gives you an extremely useful and valuable asset. You can use this list not only to inform and market to a very capable audience, you can also drive out requests to client satisfaction surveys or automate a post purchase email that asks for or even provides an incentive to leave a review for the product or service that the customer is just purchased. The third way you could get reviews on websites while that might be your own, it's more and more likely every day that users are going to be using other websites to review you, your products and or services. Your own website is of course were you have the most control over your content and you should consider creating a section devoted to testimonials and sharing the experiences of past clientele. This is an opportunity to host user generated content on your sites that search engines will love & for your users, interpretation about the genuine life experience of past patrons can be a powerful influence to the purchasing decision that a prospective customer is thinking about. And don't forget to provide an area where users can submit reviews directly on your pages. Whether you build this into your site directly or you embed one of the many third-party review solutions, you'll never get any reviews, if you don't ask. Aside from your own pages, there is an ever-growing list of sites out there that cater to collecting user reviews for all kinds of products. Entice your happy customers to write reviews on major business listing websites like Google plus local, Yahoo local, yelp, City search and more and remember that there are a host of industry-specific review sites like trip advisor for the travel sector that you want to focus on as well. You also want to note the different review sites offer diverse frameworks. While many use the recognizable five-star format others will break up ratings into different categories. Google plus local for example uses is a gap system but differentiates restaurant ratings by food to court and service on a 30 point scale. Regardless of how you get them and share them around the web reviews are great opportunities to build

Search Engine Optimization

content & reference to your pages that will assist people find you with the search engines and then help him along the path to conversion when I get there.

OPTIMIZING FOR LOCAL SEARCH

In order to get the best possible rankings in the search engines by now you know that you have to constantly create good, relevant content and then promoted and marketed around the web. When analyzing the pages of your site, Google and other search engines use a number of different signals to decide which pages show and in what order, when a user types in a search query and when we optimizing for local search, there are some specific items that you want to focus on. The first is on page optimization and content. Every page of your website should be optimized for a specific well researched keyword and you'll need to make sure that you're leveraging the important elements from a technical standpoint. You can have a look at previous videos for more details on technical SEO but a bare minimum, make sure you spend time optimizing your page title and meta-description; you're heading tags, body text and all text on each of your images. So far, this should be nothing new. But now let's talk about something specific to local search that can help you out. First your contact information is going to be especially important and there are some specific things you need to put on your contact us page and some specific ways. You can head over to schema.org/local business and browse around to find specific schema elements that make sense for your type of business. By adding some tags and explicitly defining these items through the markup to find it schema.org, you'll be telling search engines exactly what type of information each piece of text represents and remember this is just the basics, there micro format for everything from your hours of operation to the payment type to accept to industry-specific items like menus, for restaurants. At a minimum you want to make sure to include your business name address and phone number and you should also include things like your business email address, driving directions or map and a photo or two with appropriate alt text and don't forget the human visitors. You want to make it easy for them to contact and connect with you through forms and social media functionality. One more tip, your business information should always be in the bottom right-hand corner of your footer on every page. This is a very commonplace that users are conditioned to look for contact information and it will ensure that they can find your information quickly from any page of your site if they want to contact you. These days, you also have to consider the people are just searching for you on the desktop PCs anymore, but also searching with mobile devices when they're not at home or in the office and much of this on the go searching is with local intent. Having a site that looks good and functions on mobile devices is something that will not only serve you well with the search engines responding to search queries on mobile devices, but will also ensure that your users have a positive experience with you and your site regardless what device you're using. Google's GO MO program allows you to get a look at how your website looks on a mobile device and it can scan your site and make recommendations on how you can improve your pages mobile performance. If you have resources or programming expertise, you might choose to address some of these issues by creating a separate site exclusively for your mobile users on a separate domain or sub domain or better yet you might choose to use a responsive design that adapts to whatever size of screen your website is being rendered on from a single code base. If you're looking for a quick solution and you have a static website, you can take advantage of a partnership the Google has with Google mobile to create a quick and dirty mobile version of your pages right from the GO MO site. The bottom line is that many of your local customers are using mobile devices and if your site doesn't provide the information your mobile visitor needs or if it crashes or browser, you've probably lost a potential customer. Focusing on your on page optimization your contact page, proper schema markup and mobile performance will ensure that you are taking the right steps towards local search visibility with the things that you can control on the pages of your site.

How people use search engines to find places; things and businesses is in a constant state of change. As technologies improve local businesses have gained more and more ways to reach their customers and the pace of change is only going to speed up in the future. Perhaps the most explosive trends these days are social media and mobile device usage. Social media is something that's happening on the go more than ever before and a great example of social media working with mobile devices to deliver local content is Google plus local. For mobile devices using GPS or cell tower signals to become location aware, a whole new set of local functionality is unlocked. Users can use their mobile browsers or download iPhone or android apps that keep them connected to their Google plus account and write from the out, they can find local businesses based on their current location and read reviews from other Google plus users or people in the networks. You can also write reviews on the go. Share information with your social networks and even get directions to local business from wherever you happen to be by car by foot or even by public transportation. From the browser view were back home on your laptop local is now integrated right into Google plus. The important part is that this isn't something that's coming in the future all these features that we just talked about are already here. This is where things are going; your online experience is becoming more and more tailored to where you physically are and the lines between local search, social media and the kinds of devices you're using are beginning to disappear. Over and above Google plus, people are using micro blogging services like twitter on the go in a variety of devices from a variety of different apps. People are checking in to physical locations on networks like foursquare, scanning QR codes to redeem coupons or get more information about something out there in the world and their maintaining the relationships through networks like Facebook. This nearly endless stream of content can be overwhelming and new apps and new technologies are popping up every single day. Each and every one of these presents an opportunity, but the key is that you'll need to figure out which ones are applicable to your business and which ones are useful for your customers. The future local search is looking brighter than ever. Smart phones and social media are helping people discover businesses in their own town that they might have otherwise overlooked and the rapid pace at which ideas become reality promises new and innovative things in the future, you'll need to be paying attention to. To further develop your local skills and to stay up-to-date on the things that are happening in local search, make sure to keep an eye on resources like these and stay connected to your consumer base.

****

CHAPTER: 10
INTERNATIONAL SEO

The Internet allows us to find and interact with a global audience that we wouldn't have dreamed of reaching in the past. But bringing your website to people across the world present some challenges it must be considered with respect to search engines and how they view the pages of your site. A fundamental thing to remember for international SEO is that the different search engines people use in different countries can vary quite a bit. While Google and Bing might cover the majority of US-based searchers. Other countries will have different search engines altogether. Remember that search engines usually of geography specific versions of their engines designed for the different regions of the world. Everything from the layout of the search results page to the language and types of content they think is relevant for a user in a specific country can be very different across these geo-targeted search engines. The first step to getting serious about international SEO is to have your sites content translated and regionalized to the appropriate language and country combinations you are retargeting. This is going to take some time and resources and is not a place to cut corners. If you don't have the proper resources in-house there are some very good translation and interpretation services out there that will ensure that the quality of your page translations in other languages is just as higher the content written in your original language. Once you have the content translated, it's also going to be important that you create new pages on new URLs for your different language content and you provide an easy way for users to switch languages on any page of your site. It's also important to consider that although the same language can be used in different countries, there are lots of different flavors, dialects and cultural differences from country to country. If you operate in Mexico Argentina and Costa Rica you might consider having not just one translation for the Spanish language but three for the regionalized versions of each of your pages. As you put your translations and regionalized pages up, make sure to take a look at the data you'll be gathering in your web analytics solution. This is where you'll be able to see which search engines are driving what kind of traffic to which regionalized sections of your website and you can use the same fundamental measurement and optimization concepts to ensure that your finding and leveraging opportunities as well as creating and promoting content that speaks to users in their own languages.

OPTIMIZING TECHNICAL CONTENT

Structuring your website is very important for international SEO when you have different languages and localizations of your content and there are some technical things you can do to your pages to help search engines, find and understand the different internationalize sections of your website. First, determining where to place your translated content is an important step. Some organizations structure their multilingual websites by placing different translations in different sub-domains. For example you might place your Spanish version of the site on ES.your domain.com. Other websites will place the content in different subfolders like your domain.com/yes. Both methods are effective in establishing a different silo of content dedicated to a certain language and they both have risks and advantages. While using different subdomains allows you freedom and implementation, since it can be considered a completely different website, it also brings the risk of not taking advantage of the overall link value of your main domain. Using subfolders the house your multilingual content eliminates this risk and it brings the full strength of your domain to bear. But it may be challenging to implement different site frameworks this way depending upon how your e-commerce platform is set up. Next, make sure to explicitly tell search engines what language and region the content is targeted to using Hreflang link tags on your pages. These tags will tell search engine where each internationalize version of the page lives by specifying each of the URLs along with the language and country targets. So if you have one version of your page in English and another in French, you can put these two tags on both pages, specifying which URLs house each piece of content and you can be more specific by adding country targets as well. If you had one version of the page targeted to French-speaking Canadians for example, you could modify this tag to include both the language and the country code. When it's all said and done search engines will be able to properly identify what audience each page is targeted to and display the most relevant result in the different geo-targeted search engines. Also be sure to use well canonical tags on each language specific version of your content pages. This can be especially important when you have similar content targeted to different countries within the same languages. You can avoid duplication problems by explicitly calling out the unique URLs of each piece of content in each language. As long as you determine a scalable structure to house your different international content and you apply the appropriate location, language and canonical tags, search engines will have an easy way to determine which languages and countries each of your content pages are intended to serve and this will help get the most relevant and appropriate pages of your site in each of the language specific search results.

OPTIMIZING TRANSLATED AND LOCALIZED CONTENT

What we translate and localize websites content for different countries and languages, we essentially creating another website and that means that while we are leverage a lot of the work we've done for our primary language will need to go through an entire keyword and content strategy for each of the different languages were targeting. Starting with the foundation of keyword research, you want to go through this process in the language are optimizing for and come up with language specific lists of keywords that you can map to the content your translating. You can start out with translations of some of your top primary language keywords, but remember that many words and phrases don't translate directly between languages. You should expect that you'll find some interesting surprises and insights. You need to make sure that you have a native speaker of the language you're working with. But also understands the cultural aspects of the country or countries that you're targeting. Once you've done the research and have a solid understanding of your translated keywords, you'll be ready to start the translation process. The first step is mapping the pages of your site that will be translating to the appropriate keywords you will be targeting from your localize research. Once you know what keyword each of your pages will be optimized for, you'll need to ensure that whoever is doing the actual translating understands the basic principles of technical on page SEO. Titles headings and the body copy or extremely important and knowing what keywords your writing or translating for upfront will ensure that your creating content that's optimized for the right target terms, right from the beginning. Lastly, you want to evaluate whether or not you need regionalized content within a certain language. If you're doing business in the US, Canada the UK and Australia you might be able to get away with a single English version of your site. But you might not. Knowing your customers and your business along with looking at your website analytics data and consulting people who understand the cultural nuances of each region will help you determine how to write your translated content for target keywords across the different languages and whether or not to invest an additional country and language combinations.

BUILDING LINKS

Once you have your translated and regionalized pages up and live on your site along with a solid content strategy, you're ready to build links back to those pages and encourage social interactions. Link building for multilingual content follows the same rules as any other content. But there are a few things to consider as it may have some effect on your overall link building strategy. Search engines try to deliver a search experience that is relevant to users, in part based on where they are and there are certainly parts of the ranking algorithms that take regional factors into account. One way to determine map is by analyzing the back links; not just for quality and trustworthiness but they also take into consideration what region these back links are associated with. When you're seeking out link opportunities for your internationalized pages, focus on websites that operate or conduct business in the country or countries you're targeting. You can also take a look at their back links and make sure that their associated with that same region. One other side effect of search engines trying to tailor their results to people in different regions is of the top 10 search results in one country can be very different than the top 10 results in another country. When you're doing your competitive research were looking for link building opportunities, you want to make sure that you're using international versions of the search engines themselves. For example if you're looking for link opportunities for the Costa Rican Spanish version of your pages don't go to

Google.com. head over to Google.co.CR and start searching using Spanish keywords. Take a look at who's ranking for these terms now and have a look at where their back links are coming from to see if there any that you want to pursue based on the same link building principles, you'd use with any other link building activities. Last just as you'll need an expert to do your translations and regionalization; in order to do link outreach in a different country or language, you may find that you run into some barriers. If you're not comfortable with language and cultural norms of those that you're working with, you might want to consider finding a resource that is, in order to maximize the chances of turning these relationships into valuable and high-quality links link. Building for international SEO isn't that different than what you would do normally and making sure to include your translated and regionalized pages in your overall link building plan and keeping a few extra things in mind will help you with the search engines all across the globe.

SEO CAMPAIGN:

Measuring your site for international SEO is similar to what you would do with any other site, except you have to be able to segment your sites to view each language specific section of your site individually. You can measure and analyze the different international sections with your web analytics software. Using Google analytics you can filter your reports or create advanced segments to match the sub domain or subfolder structure that holds your content for each specific language. This will allow you to find insights such as e-commerce comparisons between your French and Spanish visitors or determine if certain pieces of content are more or less engaging are likely to drive conversion in one language versus another. You can also set up Webmaster tools profiles for each language specific sub domain or subfolder. This

Search Engine Optimization

will allow you to really configure and optimize your international sections differently from one another. For example you might identify crawl errors that are affecting one part of the site but not another and make sure to review any HTML suggestions for different language sections of your site and you can men is site map separately for each of your international sections as well. To view ranking data for each of your international sections, you can use tools like the SEOmaz campaigns feature. This lets you enter a list of keywords to be tracked on a specific geo-targeted search engine and it will show you how all of your international keywords perform for search engines across the world. Here, you can find out what content ranks well for certain languages and how each internationalize sections visibility improves over time. whatever KPI's you've determined to measure your SEO performance, you can look at them in the context of each regionalise section of your website and don't forget to use the geographic segments of your web analytics solution supports. You can explore which regions of the world are responding to the different languages your supporting and you can identify opportunities for expanding into additional languages or breaking existing languages into more specific regionalized versions of content. Making sure that your measurement strategy includes the international sections of your website will help you to continue to improve your performance.

AVOIDING PITFALLS:

Although, doing international SEO gives you an opportunity to find new global markets and engage with people all across the world. It can be a complicated process with plenty of pitfalls that can hurt your progress. These are some things to watch out for and will doing it the right way might take more time and resources up front. It will be worth the effort in the long run. First you are going to want to guide clear of auto translated content. All your translation technology has improved a lot over the years. It stills not nearly as good as a competent human translator that can truly interpret and craft a message that gets the point across in a way that's appropriate to our region and a culture. Auto translated content can come off as very unnatural and awkward and while some may appreciate the effort; many will view it as a negative or a clear sign that you're not serious about serving them. Another thing to watch out for is, how words and phrases are translated and used in other countries or languages. In the US an English-speaking American might search the term car insurance to get some car insurance quotes. If you were to translate this keyword phrase directly into French you might end up with this and although it's a valid translation of the phrase in French-speaking Canada, people will be more likely to use this and what if you're renting cars, if the English version of your site is talking about car rentals and you decide to expand to the UK, you better know that in London you can hire a car. just as easily as rent one. These are the nuances that you'll start to find as you do regionalized keyword research and having someone that understands your target region and language will be invaluable to you as you go through this process. Next, don't fall into the trap of just translating whatever you can, whenever you have time and slapping it up on your pages. While mixing languages on a single page is really confusing to a search engine. Even separate pages within an unclear structure can hinder the search engines ability to find and understand your content. Take the time to plan out your regionalized versions of your website and develop clear navigation that will help search engines correctly group your content by language and region. You can further help the search engines by using metadata to define language and location targeting; and spending the time and resources to go through these steps will ultimately help your international search engine visibility. Last, make sure that you really internationalize your site for the audience you're targeting. You may take the time to figure out what they call car rentals in the UK but, if it turns out that taxies, trains in the tube or the way that your customers get around in London, you really missed your audience. Just as with any business make sure that you've done the market research to truly understand the international opportunity as well as how to speak to the specific audience around the needs that your products and services are fulfilling. Your number one priority is to provide your users with the best experience possible and if you make an effort to create a quality user experience for your differentiated translated and regionalized content, it will result in improvements in your global search engine visibility.

Conclusion:

Hopefully, by now you're feeling comfortable with the basics of search engine optimization. You are probably also seen the rabbit hole of SEO and you may have been left wanting for more. If that's the case you can certainly dive deeper into any of the topics we covered or learn more about topics that we haven't. There will be lots and lots of online resources out there on SEO that can help you learn more and keep up with the latest information. The blogs and forums of SEO maws.org or fantastic place to start. We use some of the SEOmazs tools throughout this book and contribute to their content are top-notch and extremely well regarded across the industry. Wherever you go from here, I hope you gain a solid foundational knowledge of how search engines do what they do. I hope your path ahead is a little clearer and I wish you the best of luck with your search engine strategy.

****

Made in the USA
Lexington, KY
07 January 2017